Crossing Over

Residential Real Estate Agent

to

Commercial Real Estate Agent

The Ultimate Guide to Help You Become a
Successful
Commercial Real Estate Professional

First paperback edition August 2019

Graphic Design by Jenny Bijleveld
Edited by T. Alexis Waleski

ISBN 978-1-7334026-0-6 (paperback)

www.george-donohue.com

Contents

Introduction

There comes a time in everyone's life where they need or want to make a decision to alter the course of their life.

I hope this book helps you in your journey in three ways.

First to find the bridge to cross over to the world of commercial real estate. Second, to help you up and over the span. Third, to figure out which particular direction to go once you get to the other side.

There are some similarities between the livelihood of being a residential real estate agent and the profession of being a commercial real estate agent.

However, there are very many differences between the two. This book identifies all the major differences and many of the minor differences. It will explain to you clearly why these differences exist and what to participate and plan for in order to make a lucrative career in commercial real estate.

This book is also an ideal guide book for the person who is not in real estate now and is contemplating a career in real estate to help decide if they want to enter the residential or commercial real estate profession.

Chapter 1: The Life of a Commercial Real Estate Agent

The life of a commercial real estate agent is never boring. It is always filled with very interesting experiences and can be very lucrative.

A typical week can be filled with meeting business owners of all kinds of companies, conferring with investors looking for good investments and inspecting properties that are always very different and sometimes eye-opening.

Many commercial real estate agents work alone on their deals, however, many commercial real estate pros especially, in the more well-known larger firms will work on a team. These particular professionals will often spend part of their day strategizing with their team members on how to fulfill the assignments that their clients have given them.

Commercial real estate requires a bit more knowledge about contracts because there are so many ways to make money in commercial real estate. You will need to take some time and look over contracts.

One of the best parts of commercial real estate is all the types of buildings and properties you get to walk through, experience, inspect and get to know. Your imagination can help you understand the thousands of types of properties. For example, you may be asked to sell a major donut factory and will get to see how donuts are made from scratch and delivered all the way to their final destination. Or you may be asked to find a bowling alley to buy and will need to look behind the scenes on how all the contraptions work. You will tour fancy restaurants and some great Mom and Pop places. In a typical week you may need to walk through a cavernous warehouse that stores cosmetics, a hotel that caters to summer vacationers, a doctor's office, a high-tech store, an architect's office; the choices are immeasurable. In Chapter 5 we discuss the numerous types of properties you can be involved in commercial real estate.

From an intellectual point of view, you will certainly meet some very smart, capable people because your life will be filled with meeting all kinds of executives and usually spending time with the people "at the top" who are making the decisions for their companies or enterprises.

For the most part, these clients will be more decisive and be driven by their budget and business plan rather than emotions.

To find commercial clients you will be spending more time networking in both business and social settings. You will need to attend more parties, more Chamber of Commerce meetings, trade shows and business association gatherings. So, a part of your routine will be mingling with other executives and business owners. Chapter 4 goes over the many types of clients to whom you can provide services.

If you are fortunate to work in an international environment as I was when I headed up the real estate division at the first World Trade Center, you will have the great pleasure and experience of meeting people from all over the world each and every day.

In residential real estate your deals may require you to negotiate a few elements of the deal such as the purchase price, the down payment and the closing date.

The reason commercial real estate deals have such big commissions is because there are more components that need to be addressed and negotiated especially in the commercial leasing of office space and retail space. So, there will be more time spent sharpening and applying your negotiating skills.

Your schedule will be different from a residential agent. Whereas a residential agent can be a "part-timer", that is, they can work on the weekend on residential real estate and then during the week do another job, this is almost impossible in commercial real estate.

Most of the business world operates from 9 am to 5 pm Monday through Friday so this is when your clients want to meet with you, inspect properties and negotiate their deals. Similar to the clients you will be serving, you will have the weekends to yourself. This is usually the time commercial real estate professionals may do some emails, look over contracts and plan their next week's schedule.

It is difficult to work as a residential agent on the weekends and a commercial real estate agent during the week. It is possible but you need to be highly organized and have a lot of stamina. I have never seen someone be very good at both. At some time, you will need to make a decision to completely cross over.

As I mentioned in the first sentence, you can see how the life of a commercial real estate agent is never boring. It is filled with many interesting people, properties and experiences. And it is a very lucrative business.

Continue reading and learn more about the life of a commercial real estate professional to see if it is the right lifestyle for you!

The following are some well-known people who had the courage to take a chance and change their career:

Harrison Ford

Harrison Ford was born in Chicago and after dropping out of Ripton College in Wisconsin. He moved to California in 1964 with his first wife. He had a couple of unsuccessful studio contracts and worked as a carpenter to support his wife and eventually his two children. He was successful as a carpenter and had **contractor-to-the-stars** client list. When George Lucas offered him a $485-a-week part in a film called *American Graffiti*, Ford asked for a $15 raise to cover what he stood to lose by not doing carpentry for a few weeks. (PAPPADEMAS, 2013) A couple of years later he was installing some woodwork in an office when George Lucas and Brian De Palma were casting for Princess Leia and needed someone to run lines with the actresses. Ford spent several days doing lines for a part he had no expectation of getting. From getting that role it lead to all the Star Wars movies, the Indiana Jones movies and many movie and TV appearance that lead him to fame. (PAPPADEMAS, 2013)

Jeff Bezos

Jeff Bezos had a lucrative career in computer science on Wall Street and took on top roles at various financial firms before transitioning to the world of e-commerce and launching Amazon. It was 1994, and Bezos was a senior vice president at D.E. Shaw & Co., a Wall Street-based investment banking firm. Eight years out of college, Bezos was 30 years old, and while his career in finance was lucrative, he was personally unfulfilled. One year later, in July 1995, Bezos formally launched Amazon.com, and the rest is history. (Marble, n.d.)

Vera Wang

Vera Wang was a figure skater and journalist before entering the fashion industry at age 40. Today she's one of the world's premier women's designers. Vera Wang was an aspiring Olympic figure skater and realized that dream would never be full filled. She went to school in Paris and came back to the US and worked in Vogue magazine. At one point she realized her career there had no more upward mobility and she needed a new trajectory. She left Vogue and started her own fashion line.

Dwayne "The Rock" Johnson

Dwayne "The Rock" Johnson transitioned careers not once, but twice. Before he was "the most electrifying man in sports entertainment," Johnson was briefly a backup linebacker for the Canadian Football League's Calgary Stampeders. He ditched the football career and joined the World Wrestling Federation (WWF) in 1996 at 24, which catapulted him to stardom and allowed him to cross over to TV and movies in the early 2000s. (Gallett, n.d.)

Ronald Reagan

Long before Ronald Reagan became the 40th president of the United States at 69, he was a young, up-and-coming Hollywood actor in film and TV. Ronald Regan was born in Illinois and became an actor in 1937. He retired from acting in 1965 and was elected governor of California in 1966. He was elected president in 1980.

Sara Blakely

Billionaire Spanx founder Sara Blakely sold office supplies door-to-door for seven years in her 20s before her line of slimming footless pantyhose launched to success in 2000. She quit her sales job at 30 to run her company full-time. Sara Blakely was working for office supply company, Danka in Atlanta, when she need a smoothing undergarment. After two years development, she pitched SPANX to some hosiery mills in North Carolina. None of the men who she pitched to like the idea but she eventually got a call back from a mill operator who's daughters convinced him to try the concept. This lead to deals with Neiman Marcus, Bloomingdales, Saks and Bergdorf Goodman.

Chapter 2: The Differences between a Residential Agent and a Commercial Real Estate Agent

Before we begin to compare and contrast the differences between a residential agent and a commercial agent, let us look at the technical definition of what is simply an agent and what is a broker.

Real estate agents are licensed professionals who arrange real estate transactions, putting buyers and sellers together and acting as their representatives in negotiations.

In almost every state, a real estate agent must work for or be affiliated with a real estate broker (an individual or a brokerage firm), who is more experienced and licensed to a higher degree. (Chen, 2019)

A broker is an individual or firm that charges a fee or commission for executing buy and sell orders submitted by an investor. A broker also refers to the role of a firm when it acts as an agent for a customer and charges the customer a commission for its services. (Smith, 2019)

Throughout this book I will use the term agent and broker interchangeably because all the information applies to both agents and brokers.

There are many differences between residential agents and commercial agents.

A key difference between a residential pro and a commercial pro is the jargon that commercial real estate agents use.

There are special words and expressions that are used by commercial real estate agents that may be difficult for agents and others to understand. The jargon reflects that different aspects of real estate that they are involved with, in their part of the overall profession.

The most critical element to bond a tribe is language. Commercial real estate experts have their own language, their own jargon. It is important to learn the right words and the right times to use them. Using residential language will give away your "newness".

Similar to the accents of people in different parts of the United States there are certain phrases that may apply to their region.

The following are some of the phrases, nick names and abbreviations that you should learn:

A Set-up versus a Listing

In commercial real estate we do not use the phrase "listing" or "listing sheet". It sounds too residential. Commercial real estate experts will ask for the "set-up". The set up can be 1 to 20 pages. It will list all the important items for the reader to use to make a decision to consider the property. Set ups can be used for an investment property that is for sale or a space to be leased. The words "Set up" will not be on the document.

The phrase Offering Memorandum may also be used for properties that are being offered for sale. The phrase Offering Memorandum will be cited on the front page.

Inspection versus a Showing

Commercial real estate pros don't really use the term "showing". This too sounds residential. We like to say "inspection". In actual use we would say "When do you want to schedule an inspection". The term is used for anyone who is going to go see the property. It does not mean that a home inspector is going to the site.

NOI-Net Operating Income

An important calculation in investment sales is the NOI. It is an abbreviation for Net Operating Income. NOI is simply the money that is left over after the income is collected and the bills are paid. It does not take into account the debt payments. The income generally refers to the rent that is generated from tenants. It can also include other income for example parking fees, advertising from bill boards on the property, etc.

Income – Expenses = Net Operating Income

Misunderstanding the NOI can be a very dangerous situation.

I often tease newbies when they tell me how much the rental income is related to the property. I will ask them "what do you mean by rent?". They always answer; "You know, it is rent." And I will reply again; "okay but what do you mean by rent?" I keep asking until they break. I wait until they are totally exasperated and then I explain it to them. Rent can be defined as many things:

Do you mean the actual rent that is collected?

Do you mean the rent that is shown on the leases that is supposed to be collected?

Do you mean the average rent that was collected for the last 3 years?

Do you mean it is a pro forma rent? (That is a projected rent)

Do you mean the rent if the property was fully rented at 100%

Do you mean the rent with a 5% vacancy rate?

You can see how this income number can be very different depending on how you define "rent".

In regard to expenses, some commercial real estate agents can be a bit tricky. They may not list all the expenses and merely list the key expenses or they may "forget" to include all the expenses.

It is critical that you obtain all the expense information and all the backup info to support the expenses. Here is a good list of key expenses:

Real Estate Tax

Property Insurance

Liability Insurance

Electric

Heating

Water

Sewer

Garbage removal

Repairs

Maintenance

Property Management

Legal Fees

Accounting Fees

Marketing

Advertising

Telecom and internet

Security

Landscaping

Snow removal

Administration

GRM

GRM is the abbreviation for Gross Rent Multiplier. Clients who are investors like to speak in "investor short hand." They need to quickly tell their commercial real estate representative what they are looking for in regard to investing in properties.

They may couch their request by giving a direction such as; "I will only buy properties that are less than 10X GRM". What they are saying is that you should look at the ratio between what the total amount of the gross rent is each year compared to the asking price for the property.

For example, if a building has 4 apartments that generate $1,000 per month in rent, the annual rent will be $48,000. A "10 times" GRM is calculated as follows;

10 x 48,000 = $480,000.

Leasing vs. Renting

The phrase "leasing space" is more prevalent in commercial real estate. In residential real estate you use the term "rent" more often. In commercial real estate there are so many different types of leases: short-term; long-term, percentage lease, graduated lease, ground lease, sub-lease, sale-leaseback, etc.

In commercial real estate if you want to sound more professional use the verb 'lease' more often.

Buy vs. Invest

This is another subtle difference in the use of real estate jargon. In residential the verb "to buy" is more commonly used. In commercial real estate it is better to say "my clients want to invest in a property"; "she wants to make an investment", "I represent an investor".

It sounds a little sophomoric to say "My client wants to buy a good building that needs work". It is better to say; "My client is an added-value investor who wishes to invest in a Class B commercial property".

Mortgage vs Financing (Debt)

There is a difference in the way commercial real estate professionals describe different elements in the world of commercial real estate.

As mentioned, it is subtle. I am not saying that you must use certain phrases but if you use phrases that sound more "residential" it may telegraph that you are a newbie.

In residential real estate we always use the term "mortgage". What type of mortgage is the client

going to get, etc.? "My buyer's mortgage was
approved."

In commercial real estate we will use the word "debt"
and the word "financing" more often.

You will hear sentences like: "What kind of debt
service are you projecting in regard to this
investment?". "How much debt can this deal
structure handle?". "How is your client going to
finance this investment?"

Lessee vs. Renter

In commercial real estate we will never say "There
are a lot of good renters in the building". In
commercial real estate leases, you will always see the
word "lessee". Sometimes the term 'lessor".

If you have clients that are leasing space in a building
it is best to avoid calling them renters. You should
call them commercial tenants or lessees.

The word lessor is another way to say landlord or
property owner.

If a commercial tenant subleases their space to
another company, the original tenant can then be
referred to as the "sub-lessor" and the new tenant
who is subleasing the space can be referred to as the
sub-tenant.

Sales Agent vs. Managing Director

In residential real estate a majority of agents will have the title "Sales Agent" typed on their business card. Or perhaps the title "Licensed Sales Agent" or "Real Estate Salesperson".

These titles are very rare on a commercial real estate person's business card. More often you will find the title "Managing Director". In commercial real estate the agents prefer to have a more corporate sounding title. In addition, often commercial real estate pros will handle leasing assignments, advisory work, asset management, so the having the word "sales' in their title is detrimental to the image they are trying to project.

NNN Lease (Triple Net Lease)

A tripe net lease is a lease where the tenant or as commonly referred to in the lease – the lessee - agrees to pay all the real estate taxes, property insurance, and maintenance (the three different "nets" of triple net) on the property in addition to any of the typical fees that are expected under the agreement (rent, utilities, etc.).

Some commercial real estate professionals just deal in these types of leases. A good example is where a major franchise may have a free-standing building built for them and then they lease the entire building from the building owner. The franchise pays for all the bills as cited above.

They are called a triple net lease tenant and the income is just like a bond to the building owner because usually the franchise company signs a 15-year NNN lease and pays the rent and the owner does not pay any bills associated with the property. Many franchise companies have excellent creditworthiness so in all likelihood they will pay their rent every month on time for 15 years just like a bond.

Net Absorption

Net absorption is a calculation that commercial real estate experts monitor. It basically is taking the units of something that the market "takes" minus the units of something that the market has not taken.

Net absorption gives you insight into the supply and demand of a particular type of real estate in a particular market.

For example, in office leasing it is the total amount of space that tenants physically moved into minus the total amount of space that tenants physically moved out.

It is essentially the measurement of the net change of the supply of commercial space in a given real estate market over a specific period of time. It is measured by deducting commercial space vacated by tenants and made available on the commercial space market from total space leased up.

Negative Net Absorption means that more commercial space was vacated or in other words was put onto the market more than what was leased up or absorbed by the commercial tenants. Under negative Net Absorption scenario, the commercial rents would tend to decrease or cool down.

Positive net absorption just means that there was more space leased up than was put onto the market. Rents usually rise in a positive net absorption environment.

Cap Rate

Cap rate is short for the term Capitalization Rate.

It is a tool that helps brokers, investors and bankers evaluate an investment. It is used to compare one investment against another or others.

It gives you insight into the potential rate of return of an investment.

The higher the cap rate, the better for the investor.

It is something that should never be used just by itself to determine if an investment is a good one or not. There are quite a few other factors and elements to consider when investing in real estate.

There are 3 things presented in the cap rate formula:

The Net Operating Income

The Value of the Property

The Cap Rate itself.

Here is one way to look at the evaluation:

Cap Rate $=$ Net Operating Income
Current Value of the Building

You can also utilize the cap rate as follows:

Value = Net Operating Income
Cap Rate

So, a commercial real estate investor may ask a broker to find a property that "throws off" a 7% cap rate. So, a commercial broker will calculate the data of various properties for sale to see if they equate to a 7% cap rate.

For example, if a property had a Net Operating Income of $36,000 per year and you divide that by .07 (which is 7%) the value of the building should be $514,286.

In other words, this particular investor will **NOT** want to pay more than $514,286 for this property.

It is also important to note that not all investors are alike. Perhaps during a particular market cycle one investor may desire 7% cap rate investments, another may want 6%, and another may want 6.75% and so forth.

Investors are always looking at what else can they do with their money. What else may be able to "throw off" or generate a better return? It could be stocks, or bonds, or artwork, etc. So, their decision about what Cap Rate they prefer is based on what else they can do with their money.

ROI

ROI is another well know abbreviation in commercial real estate. It stands for Return on Investment.

The ROI measures how much money (or the profit) is made on an investment as a percentage of the cost of the investment.

It shows how well the investment dollars are being used to generate profits.

To calculate the profit on any investment, you would take the total return on the investment and subtract the original cost of the investment.

However, ROI is a ratio. It gives us the profit on an investment represented in percentage terms.

To calculate the percentage return on investment, we take the net profit or net gain on the investment and divide it by the original cost.

$$\text{Rate of Investment} = \frac{\text{(Profit on the Investment -- Cost of the Initial Investment)}}{\text{Cost of the Initial Investment}}$$

Let's look at the ROI in regard to an all cash transactions. This means you buy the property with all cash. There is no mortgage. No financing involved.

You pay $200,000 in cash for the rental property.

The closing costs were $5,000, and some repairs costs totaled $10,000, bringing the total investment to $215,000 for the property.

You collected $2,000 in rent every month.

At the end of the year you want to calculate your return

You earned $24,000 in rental income for that year.

Expenses, including the water bill, property taxes, and insurance, totaled $10,000 for the year

Your <u>annual return</u> was $14,000 ($24,000 - $10,000 = $14,000).

To calculate the property's ROI:

Divide the annual return ($14,000) by the amount of the total investment or $215,000.

ROI = $14,000 ÷ $215,000 = 0.065

The return on your total investment (the ROI) was 6.5%

Defining ROI when Financing is Involved

Now let's say instead of an all cash deal you want to get a mortgage or in other words finance the investment. Your ROI is going to be higher because you are using less of YOUR cash to make the investment.

Calculating the ROI on transactions where a mortgage or financing is part of the deal is more involved.

For example, you purchased the $200,000 property as cited above, but instead of paying cash, you took out a mortgage.

The down payment needed for the mortgage is 30% of the purchase price or $60,000 ($200,000 sales price x 30% = $60,000).

Closing costs for the mortgage required $2,500 up front.

You paid $10,000 for renovations.

Your total <u>expenses</u> were $72,500 ($60,000 plus $2,500 plus $10,000).

There are also ongoing costs with a mortgage:

Let's assume you took out a loan and your monthly payment is $500.

Add the same $10,000 per year regarding the water bill, taxes, insurance.

Rental income of $2,000 per month totals $24,000 for the year.

Your cash flow is:

Rental Income minus (Water, Taxes, Insurance and Mortgage Payments) equals Net Annual Return

Rental Income		$24,000
Water, Taxes, Insurance	$10,000	
Mortgage Payments	$6,000	

	Total	$16,000	($16,000)
Net Annual Return			**$8,000**

To calculate the property's ROI:

Divide the net annual return by the original out-of-pocket expenses (the down payment of $60,000, closing costs of $2,500 and remodeling for $10,000) to determine the ROI.

ROI: $8,000 ÷ $72,500 = 11%

ROI is 11%.

CAM

CAM stands for Common Area Maintenance. It is most commonly found in the world of shopping centers.

The way shopping center owners calculate their Common Area Maintenance can vary very widely because so many things can be added in.

Here is a short list of some of the items that can be included in CAM:

Repairs

Insurance

Property Management

Salaries of Admin staff

Property Taxes

Landscaping

Parking Lot Stripes

Security

Utilities

Snow Removal

The CAM charges can be quite complicated and very expensive.

Tenants will pay their proportionate share of the CAM charges depending on how big their store is. The CAM charges are usually billed as a per square foot charge.

Tenant Rep

A Tenant Rep is short for Tenant representative. It basically means that you primarily represent the tenants of buildings. You can represent retail tenants or office tenants. You find space for them to lease and then negotiate on their behalf against the landlord. You may also negotiate the renewal of a tenant's lease so they can remain in the property with hopefully newer, better terms.

Landlord Rep

A landlord rep is short for a Landlord's Representative. Landlord reps are commercial real estate professionals that work for the landlord and they can negotiate all the leases related to the landlord's building or portfolio of buildings. Landlord's representatives conduct the marketing of the vacant spaces, find tenants, and negotiate the leases. Most often, their primary goal is to lease up the entire building with great, creditworthy tenants at the best lease rates.

USF and RSF

USF and RSF are abbreviations for Useable Square Feet and Rentable Square feet.

RSF is tricky tactic where the landlord is able to obtain rent for every single square inch of space in the building.

USF is sometimes referred to as "carpetable square feet" or the actual square footage. In other words, it is the space that the tenant can actually use.

RSF take into account all the other spaces that are not in the tenant's space and adds it back into the USF.

For example, the fire stairway, the lobby, the bathrooms in the hallway, the hall way itself, etc. The tenants all pay a proportionate share of these "other" spaces.

Sometimes the RSF is 20% to 50% greater than the USF.

The problem for the tenant is that they pay their rent based on the RSF!

Let's look at an example.

A tenant is seeking to rent 10,000 square feet of space because this is the square footage, he actually needs to accommodate his office staff. This is called the USF.

The broker explains to the tenant that the particular building they are looking for has a 20% loss factor.

This means that if the tenant really wants to use 10,000 square feet, he has to agree to lease a space that is 12,500 <u>rentable square feet.</u>

12,500 multiplied by 20% = 2,500 feet.

12,500 rentable square feet – 2,500 feet = 10,000 useable square feet.

How did the landlord come up with this additional square footage?

A typical scenario could be as follows:

Let's say that the tenant is taking up half the floor and the following are other areas on that floor:

Hallways and Lobby:	2,000 square feet
Public Bathrooms:	2,000 square feet
Janitor's Storage Closet:	1,000 square feet
Total	**5,000 square feet**

There is 5,000 square feet of other space on the floor. Since you occupy 50% of the floor the landlord "artificially" adds another 2,500 square feet to your office space (50% of 5,000 square feet is 2,500 square feet).

In essence, the landlord is getting rent on every square foot on that floor

LOI and MOU

LOI is an abbreviation for Letter of Intent. MOU is an abbreviation for Memorandum of Understanding.

They can also be referred to as Term Sheets or Proposals. They all mean the same thing in spirit. It is a document that has the material terms and conditions for a proposed deal before the actual final legal document is prepared for signatures.

Cash on Cash

Cash on cash is another phrase that investors use to explain to a commercial real estate agent what type of property they are looking to invest in.

The phrase cash on cash means the ratio between the cash flow that the property is "throwing off" or generating to the cash that was invested.

It looks like this:

Cash on cash = <u>Annual cash flow (this is before taxes)</u>

Amount of cash that was invested

So, if you were going to purchase a $500,000 property and the following items were related to the purchase:

You put down $100,000
Your monthly payments for the mortgage are $2,000 per month ($24,000 annually)
<u>After all the expenses are paid</u>; the rent from the tenants is $40,000 per year

You would calculate the cash-on-cash as follows;

$$\text{Cash on cash} = \frac{\$16,000}{\$100,000}$$

Cash on cash is 16%

Investors will give instructions to a commercial real estate agent something like; "I will consider looking at investments that have a cash on cash ratio of 15% or higher". The property in the above example is something the investor would take a look at further.

Proforma

In Latin the phrase pro form means "as a matter of form" or "for the sake of form".
In commercial real estate it is a method in which to project financial assumptions.
In a pro forma analysis you may need to project what kind of revenue will be generated from the rent that the tenants may pay in the future.

You may need to project how many square feet will need to be built if it is a new construction development or needs to be renovated if it is a renovation project.

How many houses will be built, how many rooms will the hotel have, how many seats will the new restaurant accommodate, etc.

OPEX

OPEX is an abbreviation for Operating Expenses. These are the expenditures that a property owner needs to pay for to continually operate and maintain the building. It is all the day to day expenses of running the property. This includes maintenance, utilities, salaries, etc.

It does not include taxes or debt.

CAPEX

The term CAPEX is short for Capital Expenses. CAPEX are the expenditures used to acquire a property, make major upgrades or major repairs to a property.

If it is an expense that extends the life of the property then it should be categorized as CAPEX not OPEX.

HVAC

HVAC is simply defined as Heating Ventilation and Air Conditioning.

There are many ways to heat a commercial property. Buildings can use HVAC systems that use natural gas as a fuel, or oil or electricity.

Some large building use dual-fuel systems where the building can use natural gas or oil depending on which is cheaper at the time.

Air conditioning can be provided throughout out the building by duct works or similar to residential it can be provided by small units that go in the window or through the wall.

Hair on the Deal

The phrase "hair on the deal" is often used by commercial real estate pros when they are describing a real estate investment situation that may have some complications to it. For example, maybe, the building is half finished because the builder ran out of money or perhaps it has some environmental issues such as asbestos in it.

The origin of the phrase is a little ambiguous and no one really knows for certain. My feeling is that a deal that has hair on it means that it is not a smooth deal, that the hair makes it a bit messy and not so easy to see or deal with.

Some investors actually love deals with "hair on them" because they believe they may be able to get it for a lower price and they may have the solution, creativity and/or manpower to correct the issues and make bring value to the property.

Fair Housing

Another important difference between Residential Real Estate and Commercial Real Estate is that in Residential Real Estate the agents need to know more about Fair Housing and various discrimination laws.

In essence, a landlord must rent a space or sell a home to whomever is financially qualified. They cannot consider their race, religion, sexual orientation, etc.

In commercial real estate it is different because usually companies are the legal entities leasing a space and there are many factors that need to be considered to permit a company to lease space.

The law looks at residential clients as "unsophisticated". This does not mean they are <u>not</u> smart. This does not mean they do <u>not</u> know how to dress fashionably. It simply means that they may not be knowledgeable about legal issues. That they do not have a law degree, that they do not have a Legal Department that reports to them.

Commercial clients are characterized as "sophisticated" entities. This means that companies are knowledgeable about contracts, the legal process, the legal terms and requirements. Many owners of commercial companies have college degrees in which they took a legal course and many companies have in-house lawyers or law departments.

Teamwork

Another important difference between residential and commercial real estate brokerage is the use of teamwork.

Teamwork is a significant social construct encountered in various occupational, educational, and recreational settings. Efficacious teamwork is significant to increasing group effectiveness and efficiency in achieving a common goal, and also in revealing the validity of one's social skills. The coalition of individuals to adequately complete a task in a timely manner constitutes the synergy of teamwork. When working as a team the members are encouraged to use critical thinking skills in their problem-solving.

Teamwork requires communication skills in order to express one's ideas to the group. Teams also benefit from individuals with a strong sense of self-analysis. Teamwork is most efficient when the members are capable of identifying their own strengths and weaknesses. Tasks are delegated most efficiently when the decisions are influenced by the strengths of the members.

Group participation is an indicator of one's ability to work well with others. The use of proper social skills greatly increases the likelihood of systematically addressing the task at hand. Effectiveness and efficiency are significantly impacted by the communication of the group. When appropriate social interactions are observed the importance of teamwork is admissible through a complete collaboration achieving a goal which would have been daunting or required additional time if addressed by only one individual.

Gunslinger vs. Team Approach

In residential real estate the agents predominantly work on their own. They do their own research, marketing, solicitations, meeting clients, touring homes, etc. There are a few reasons for this. Most influencing is the fact that the commissions on a typical home are too small to share with another agent.

Also, to sell a home really only requires one good professional to handle everything from A to Z.

In commercial real estate it is a common practice that a team of real estate professionals will work on one transaction. The reason for this is that commercial real estate deals are usually more complex than a house deal and as explained in the previous chapters requires a broad set of skills and tools. In addition, the owners of a commercial real estate company know that a commercial client is truly a repeat customer. Commercial customers come back to their real estate experts much more often than a typical home owner in the United States. According to the National Association of Realtors that the typical American family stay in their home for 9 years and increase of almost 50% since 2008. This means that a homeowner may use a broker to sell their home but then may not need them unto 10 years later! This information is from a website called (How long do people stay in their home?, n.d.).

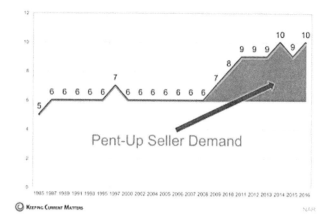

(How long do people stay in their home?, n.d.)

Commercial customers are constantly changing. A company is a very dynamic enterprise. For example, they may be expanding, or downsizing, or buying other companies. If an engineering company land a new big client, they may need to hire more people and as a result need to expand their office.

If a retail store's sales start to slide downward, they may need to reduce their store's square footage to save rent.

Since commercial real estate customers are easily repeat customers, the owners of the commercial real estate company want to be sure the commercial client is being taken care of constantly. If they have just one agent working on the assignment and that one agent becomes sick or leaves the company it can greatly put the retainage of that client in great jeopardy. The team approach assures everyone that the client will always be attended to.

Commercial real estate teams are usually comprised of people who have an expertise in one area over another area. The team leader will be the most knowledgeable and probably have the most years of experience. One team member may be very good with calculations and will handle all the spreadsheets or commonly referred to as "running the numbers". Another member usually the newest on the team will handle the showings and distribution of marketing material to prospects.

The downside of the team approach is that you will have to split the commission with other team members. So, it is important to be on a productive team. Teams that are efficient, competent and well sought after will do many deals in one year. Even though you may be the "newbie" on the team and receive a lower split you will gain more income by the team doing numerous deals.

When you are a residential real estate agent you normally have to go out and get your own clients. No one hands them to you on a silver platter. But when you are added as the newbie to a commercial real estate team that is exactly what happens. You begin working on clients your team members already cultivated and obtained.

There are many ways a commercial real estate team can divide up the commission split. Here is just one way the commission could be split on a 3-person team:

Let's say the real estate company has a commission split agreement with the Team leader where the Team Leader receives 60% of every commission and the real estate company receives 40%:

The Team may split the 60% as follows:

The Team Leader:	30%
The Second in Command:	20%
The Newbie:	10%

If you are good negotiator (Note: It is highly recommended you read <u>Real Estate Deal Making: A Property Investor's Guide to Negotiating</u>) you may be able to negotiate with the Team Leader that if you bring in a new client into the team that the commission split would then be:

The Team Leader:	25%
The Second in Command:	15%
The Newbie:	20

It is a natural progression in a commercial real estate company for the newbie to work up to the Team Leader position especially if the Team Leader retires.

Or the newbie can gain enough experience to leave the team and create their own team.

Another common methodology of working is that a commercial real estate agent may team up with a specific agent when he or she does an office deal and perhaps a different agent on a shopping center deal. That is perfectly normal and legal to do so.

3.   **Leadership**

There is a trend observed within residential real estate that is virtually absent among the world of commercial agents. The topic to be discussed: emotional influence!

In the world of residential real estate, it is common for agents to find their client's purchases to be

42

intertwined with a desire for emotional fulfillment. What does this mean? That residential clients are shopping with the expectation of an experience that will bring them emotional gratification.

Residential agents will lend focus to features that sell a home. These points of interest prove to be significantly dissimilar from those which corporate managers invite the merchandising of when traversing commercial spaces. In comprehending the partition of real estate it is arguably most important to enshrine the variance in purpose between the home buyer and the property investor. It has been established that the residential client is seeking some emotional fulfillment in the foundation of a home. Commonly, potential home owners are driven to the decision to purchase a home by a life progression such as marriage or the welcoming of a new baby.

These motivations are accompanied by imaginations of preferred structural elements that embolden their sense of "family living." The preferences described by residential clients serve to express their personal feelings of what defines "just a house" from their "future home." With this understanding of residential clients it can be inferred they are unlikely to anticipate earning any profit from their purchase. The residential client does not maintain an interest in procuring revenue.

However, when a commercial client assesses an investment property their primary concern is driven by the potential for profit. The commercial agent is responsible with presenting the client an environment which fosters economic growth for the company. The tactics relied on in commercial real estate are strategic and rational. The only preconceived ideations of commercial investors are found in concern for the efficiency of office space and consistency of capital. Their leading questions involve how much money they can make through their investments. In summary of this significant contrast, commercial investors desire properties which generate cold, hard cash, while residential clients beseech a warm, comfortable haven.

The desire for an atmosphere invoking sentiment prompts warm descriptive language from residential agents, which are foreign in the commercial sector. Common phrases heard by home buyers refer to "charming and sun-drenched" or "quaint and cozy" environments, using descriptions to appeal to the buyer's impassioned inclinations. In contrast, commercial agents have an affinity for terminology pleasant to commercial investors. When observing an interaction between the two sophisticated parties it is not uncommon to articulate a phrase such as "recurrent and predictable income." Statements as such are made to assure investors their expenditures will substantiate fruitful accounts. Rather than engaging in emotional choices the rational decision making of commercial investors is decided by determinants of efficiency and productivity. They are looking for answers to questions such as "How many people will fit in this space?", "How quickly can we be moved in and be functional?", and "How will this environment foster coworker relations and job proficiency?"

Oftentimes the irrational nature of residential shoppers permits the supposition that the "right home" will be one revered among all family members. This ideology is the bane of financial security for many residential agents. Large commissions can be squandered by dissenting assessments. Properties which rationally suit the needs of the buyer may be surpassed in an attempt to address picky concerns.

How about an example?

Emotions Killed the Deal and a $600,000 Commission.

Amidst an impressive and uncommon real estate opportunity, one residential agent, expecting a 6% commission on a $10,000,000 apartment in N.Y.C., lost the deal in its finalization by virtue of abhorrent emotional decisions. The couple involved in the transaction had professed the home's perfection and decided to continue toward purchasing. When the couple brought their two ten-year-old sons to view the home the boys exclaimed their dissatisfaction with aspects of the apartment. Their objections raised doubt and lowered emotional certainty amongst the adults. Capitulating to their emotions, the couple backed out of the deal offering no rational reason. Their abandonment of the transaction resulted in a $600,000 loss of anticipated profit for the residential agent. Sensitivity manipulated ideals tend to be an obstacle faced exclusively by residential agents.

Families, couples and individuals alike all share a common exaction. There is an ever-present need for space. When working in residential environments the clients encountered tend to be involved with different hobbies and life activities which require room for storage and practice. Finding a home with the "perfect" amount of space elicits a positive emotional reaction from clients. This being understood, "spacious" has become another catchword of the residential agent. Contrarily, CEO's interested in commercial investment share a different compilation of concerns. They are most often in search of an office space which will allow for maximum efficiency. Their interests include assessment of the most possible people per square foot that can be fit inside, and how the available area will provide to the hierarchy of the office. In commercial real estate, clients will show an appreciation for the smallest available space which retains functionality and promotes productivity.

The Hierarchy of Needs.

The ideology of real estate respective to hierarchy is expressed minimally through the residential sector. Home buyers may express their hierarchical needs through an expectation of the master suite being larger than the other bedrooms, or having a more favorable position within the structure of the home.

When assessing the corporate hierarchy of commercial real estate one must remember an individual's company prestige is reflected by their office space. It is common for the president of a corporation to have the largest, most immediate office space. Going down the chain of command one would typically find the vice president in the next office, closest to their president; then managers in large cubicles and clerks in smaller cubicles. The hierarchy is an important consideration when addressing the spatial needs of a commercial investor.

Tina Sussex Story

One of my most favorite stories that exemplifies the difference between residential real estate brokerage and commercial real estate brokerage is the Story of Tina.

Another highlight of my career was being the President of the Commercial Real Estate Division of a famous real estate company on Madison Avenue off 57th Street in Manhattan New York. Incidentally this corner was the most expensive street for retail real estate in America.

The company also had a Residential Real Estate Division and within the company was a wonderful woman named Tina. I believe she was about 50 years old and was a successful residential agent for 20 years and approached me one day and asked if she could "cross over" into commercial real estate. I knew she was hard-working, dedicated and always acted professionally so I thought she would do well.

I told her that I would first give her some one-on-one training where she could learn the basics before I handed her a client. After 3 months of Tina attending our sales meetings and the personal training, I thought she was ready to conduct her own tour of a new office space with a prospective client.

That week when I thought she was ready a client of mine called seeking a new office space for his advertising firm. He was the President of the firm and he asked me to find a new HQ space for him and if I could arrange for his C-suite entourage to join us on the inspection.

I broke the good news to Tina that she would have a new client and that she would have to manage the logistics of arranging the inspection. I urged Tina to do a preview, that is, to go and inspect the space at least a day prior to the event.

Doing a preview of a single-family home is quite easy because you have the address one and you can easily find it using your GPS. When you need to be the tour guide and show a group of executives a new space you better know exactly who to see at the building, what elevator to take, what hallway to go down, where to make the turns, how to open the space, etc. So, on the day of the inspection with the client you will be very confident and the client will know that you really know the building you are trying to convince him to lease.

On the day of the tour the five executives which included the President, the Director of Human Resources, the Chief Financial Officer, the Director of Operations and the Director of Public Relations, congregated in the main lobby. The introductions and explanation of everyone's role in the company took almost ten minutes. Tina and I took the group into the elevator and up to the space.

I told Tina it was her show but I would be standing in the background if she needed me.

She led them into the space and stopped them right inside the front door in the reception area. The group naturally fell into a semi-circle looking towards Tina. She asked for their attention and then began:

"Again, thank you for joining us today. This is a fantastic space. Before we see the rest of the space, I would like point out this wonderful coat closet. It is about 8 feet long and has room for lots of coats and bags and enough room for boots on the closet floor. It has 2 great sliding doors."

I couldn't believe my ears that she was talking so much about the coat closet. The President of the company was looking at me and giving me the 'Is she for real?" look.

I had to save this deal.

I blurted out quickly "Oh Tina is always joking, follow me gents I will give you a tour of this great space!".

We almost lost this big commission because the habits of a residential agent. It was engrained in Tina's mind and soul to always show the client the closets and to accentuate how great they are. Because to new home buyers especially buyers who have children, closets are very important. In commercial real estate the closets are absolutely not important.

Tina's story is a lesson all residential real estate agents can learn from.

Differences between residential and commercial real estate are identified in their contrasting areas of interest. Kitchens and bathrooms are areas of significant variance between the two domains. Residential agents are aware that the kitchen is most commonly the first room of the home to be examined. The kitchen is thought to be at the heart of family life. At the center of the home, residential agents will rely heavily on the kitchen to provoke an emotional response from the client.

In commercial real estate there is very little interest in kitchens. There is no rationality in focusing on a kitchen for an office space or new shopping center. CEO's are comfortable with staff relying on outside sources at meal time, and they retain the option to install a pop-up style kitchenettes. This trend is continued in examination of client interest in bathrooms. Residential agents will be bombarded with inquiries pertaining to topics such as water quality and purity, water pressure, laundry units, vanity sizes, toilet placement and shower size. Commercial agents will not be concerned with any of these queries. Oftentimes bathrooms are located in the hallways of buildings where office spaces are rented.

Understanding this is a key factor in understanding the vast differences between residential and commercial real estate. Bathrooms, a significant factor in eliciting the emotional response which encourages purchases of the residential world, are so far removed from the commercial scope of interest that oftentimes they're not even situated within the leased space.

The Bureau of Labor Statistics in 2018 reports a median yearly income just over $48,690 for all real estate agents and $58,210 for higher-trained real estate brokers, but its statistics are generally skewed toward residential real estate sales ((Real Estate Brokers and Sales Agents, n.d.). Most sources indicate that commercial real estate agents earn somewhere around $85,000 annually. Keep in mind that these figures vary, as most real estate agents' incomes are based on commissions and the geographic area where their properties are sold.

Higher-priced sales and repeat business, along with a credible reputation, typically bring commercial real estate agents larger commissions and higher yearly incomes. In general, income variability can be organized into regions in the United States often Metropolitan areas and non-metropolitan. In Metropolitan areas the median income of real estate agents is much higher, and in 2018 the NY metro area the income was $104,180. However in Northeast South Carolina non-metropolitan area the median income is $43,080.

In Los Angeles-Long Beach-Anaheim metro area the median income in 2018 is $72,160 and Midland Texas has one of the highest median incomes for realtors in the country at $111,560. While West Tennessee non metro area $27,590 has one of the lowest median income. (Occupational Employment and Wages, May 2018, n.d.) As you can see the income varies widely by location.

Chapter 3: Tools of the Trade

Tools of the Trade

The tools of the trade for commercial real estate professionals are very different than a residential agent. There are some similar tools but there are quite a few different ones. You will also need a different set of skills which can easily be obtained with the right training, mentorship, in-the-field experience and reading the right guide books.

Here is a list of the basic tools and skills you will need:

Blue Print Reading

Blue Print Reading is an essential skill to have if you want to be a commercial real estate expert. It is not necessary to be a full-fledged licenses architect but it will come in very hand if you can read the basics of blue print reading.

> The blueprinting process was developed in the mid-1800s, when scientists discovered that *ammonium iron citrate* and *potassium ferrocyanide* created a photosensitive solution that could be used for reproducing documents.
>
> The process goes like this: Someone creates a drawing on translucent tracing paper or cloth. The drawing is placed

over a piece of blueprinting paper, which has been coated with a mix chemicals. When the two papers are exposed to a bright light, the two chemicals react to form an insoluble blue compound called blue ferric ferrocyanide (also known as Prussian Blue), *except* where the blueprinting paper was covered, and the light blocked, by the lines of the original drawing. After the paper is washed and dried to keep those lines from exposing, you're left with a negative image of white (or whatever color the blueprint paper originally was) against a dark blue background.

The technique was faster and more cost-effective than hand-tracing original documents, and caught on as an easy, inexpensive way to reproduce drawings and texts. After carbon copying and copier machines took on that job for smaller documents, architects, engineers and shipwrights continued to use blueprinting to copy their large-scale drawings. More recently, the diazo whiteprint process and large-format xerographic photocopiers have largely replaced blueprinting even for these specialized purposes, and many "blueprints" are now black or grey lines on a white background. Xerograph just doesn't have the same ring as *blueprint* for a shorthand description for a master plan, though. (Soniak, 2012)

Knowing a few of the blueprint symbols will make looking at the schematic of the buildings that you are trying to lease or sell will make the plans not look like hieroglyphs and the job that much easier.

Here are some basic symbols:

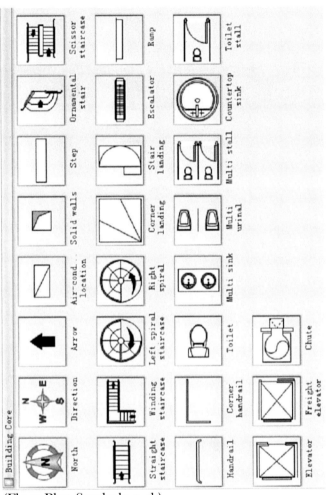

(Floor Plan Symbols, n.d.)

56

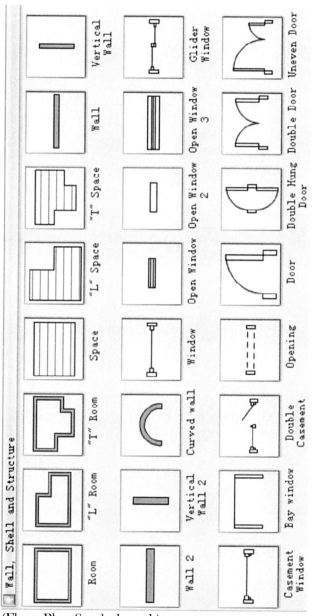

(Floor Plan Symbols, n.d.)

57

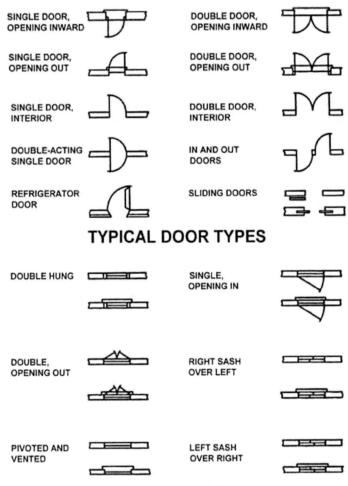

SINGLE DOOR, OPENING INWARD

DOUBLE DOOR, OPENING INWARD

SINGLE DOOR, OPENING OUT

DOUBLE DOOR, OPENING OUT

SINGLE DOOR, INTERIOR

DOUBLE DOOR, INTERIOR

DOUBLE-ACTING SINGLE DOOR

IN AND OUT DOORS

REFRIGERATOR DOOR

SLIDING DOORS

TYPICAL DOOR TYPES

DOUBLE HUNG

SINGLE, OPENING IN

DOUBLE, OPENING OUT

RIGHT SASH OVER LEFT

PIVOTED AND VENTED

LEFT SASH OVER RIGHT

TYPICAL WINDOW TYPES

(BLUEPRINTS AND CONSTRUCTION DRAWINGS: A UNIVERSAL LANGUAGE, 2011)

58

Here are some good examples, of why it will help you in your deals. Let's say you are representing a company seeking an office space to rent and the client wants to know if the office layout can accommodate 20 senior employees, 10 junior employees, a receptionist, a kitchen and 2 conference rooms.

It will be very expeditious if you can quickly review the plan and using a simple ruler give the client a yes or no answer.

Another example, is if you represent a developer or builder and they are seeking land to build a new apartment complex. You will need to be able to understand the basic zoning, possible setbacks, height restrictions, etc. A setback is a term used in land use regulations. It is the minimum distance that a building or structure must be "set back" from the property line, street or the edge of a river or a flood plain. There may be other set back lines related to fencing, landscaping, septic tanks and other structures that may be found on a property. Federal, State and Local governments all have laws or ordinances that dictate the details of the setbacks.

In regard to retail clients, you may have a client that wants to lease a restaurant space that can accommodate 45 tables with 4 chairs at each table. Knowing how to read a floor plan will help you to answer these questions.

In the beginning of a deal it may be too premature for a client to call in an architect because they may have to start paying them a hefty $/hour fee. In addition, in the beginning of the search for the perfect space for your client you may be looking at many spaces and the client is definitely not going to have the architect look at every single possibility. You bring in the architect when you have narrowed the search.

You can learn about blue print reading by taking a course at a local college or perhaps paying an architect to give you a private lesson.

Understanding Demographics

In residential real estate the client may ask about demographics which is statistical data of the population in a particular locale. They sometimes do this to see if they will fit into the culture of the area. Residential real estate agents know that they cannot use demographics in a discriminatory manner. Talking about demographics in residential real estate is very sensitive.

In commercial real estate it is totally different because retail tenants want to talk about demographics in a very positive way.

For example, if a retail tenant wants to open a women's dress shop in a particular area, they will ask you if the demographics fit their product line. For example, their dresses may be modestly priced targeting women between the ages of 18 and 25.

They want to know how many women fit into that age group, what is their average income, are they single, do they have disposable income, etc.

Demographic reports are fairly easy to read. There are companies that specialize in demographic information where you can buy individual reports.

Excel Spreadsheets

Excel is the most popular software to present a mathematical analysis related to any type of real estate transaction.

It is part of the Microsoft Office Suite of products. It is an essential tool and you should have it installed on your laptop and your phone.

There are 2 key reasons to be adept at creating spreadsheets:

1. You will be asked to do an analysis of the possible transaction.
2. You will receive analyses from the opposing party, from your clients, from other brokers, etc. and you will need to be able to decipher them.

There are a few ways to learn how to use Excel:

1. Check your local college, many offer classes specifically on Excel.

2. There are many books and online tutorials, even YouTube has a lot of videos of software usage.

3. Check with your local library, they may offer classes in their community space, or they will have books and online resources to learn many programs.

Contract Law

Residential Real Estate agents typically only need to know some basic legal documents, for example, a term sheet, a Contract of Sale, a 2-page residential apartment lease, etc.

Most of the time with residential agents they actually do a "hand off" to the lawyers.

In Commercial Real Estate it is very different.

Commercial leasing is a very lucrative part of commercial real estate deal making. However, the commercial lease can easily be 30 pages and some even more than 100 pages. It is the commercial real estate deal maker's responsibility to negotiate all of the key clauses in these very large leases.

Construction and Architecture

Basic knowledge of construction and architecture of commercial real estate properties will be invaluable during your career as a commercial real estate professional.

When you are a residential agent it is important that you understand the basics of construction especially house heating and plumbing. For example, a residential client expects you to know if a house has a natural gas-fired boiler versus an oil burner. You may be asked how many gallons the hot water tank holds.

In regard to architecture, a residential agent should be able to distinguish between a Victorian home and split-level ranch.

In commercial real estate, your knowledge of construction and architecture will need to be more comprehensive.

For example, if you are going to concentrate on office tenants, that is, representing companies that utilize office space and helping them to find a new office to lease and move into, you will need to know more than just how the office space will be heated.

In commercial leasing the commercial real estate agent is often required to negotiate what is referred to as a "Work Letter", or a "Landlord's Contribution" or a "Tenant Improvement" package. These three phrases all mean the same concept.

Basically, the Landlord and Tenant agree that the Landlord is going to give some value to have the office space designed and built out to the Tenant's specifications.

To negotiate and calculate this Work Letter, you will need to know items such as:

- how many cubicles can fit into the space,
- what kind of internet is available,
- where is the HVAC system,

- how is it controlled, who pays for the HVAC,
- is there a fire sprinkler system,
- where is the water supply line if the tenant wants to install a kitchenette,
- where is the fire egress in case of a fire,
- does the HVAC run after 6 pm; if not how does the Tenant get HVAC

Evaluating the Value of a Commercial Property

Evaluating the Value of a Commercial Property is one of the most critical skills you will need to be highly competent, successful and well-respected.

In residential real estate, agents most commonly use comparable sales in the area ('comps") to come up with the value of a property.

There are three methods in which to evaluate a property to come up with its value.

The following is a brief overview of the three approaches or what I refer to as "philosophies":

The Comparable Philosophy

The Comparable Philosophy or Approach is a concept that is predominate in residential real estate. Most residential real estate agents focus on this one approach to determine the value of a house.

It is also the concept that most lay people or typical homeowners have heard of or are most familiar with. Comparables are commonly referred to as "Comps".

Basically, this philosophy is:

To compare a group of other similar things to determine the value of the subject thing.

That "thing" can be any type of home, for example, a single-family home, a condominium or a cooperative apartment.

In commercial real estate this philosophy is also used. You select a group (say 3) of similar commercial properties in proximity to the subject property and you take the average price of each property that was recently sold for and it will give you one estimate of the value.

The big flaw with this philosophy is that the person who is conducting the valuation can choose whatever recent sales that he/she wants to choose.

In other words, the old adage, "Liars figure and figures lie" can easily be applied here.

If the agent doing the calculation wants to have a result where the value is high, the agent can easily choose the 3 highest sales and take their average.

If the agent wants to come up with a low figure, the agent can simply choose 3 recent low-priced sales and take their average.

It is obvious where the flaw is in this method.

The Income Philosophy

The Income Philosophy or Approach is more scientific than the Comparable Approach.

This Philosophy is:

To take the income and expenses of a "thing" and calculate the net income (the profit) and then apply a universally agreed to formula to the net income to determine the value of the "thing".

The thing can be any type of property. It can also be used to calculate a single-family home in which you intend to live. In this case, you would calculate what income (rent) someone would pay you to rent the house. You then deduct the expenses to operate the house. This does <u>not</u> include the mortgage.

The tricky part of this philosophy is what formula to use. In commercial real estate we refer to this formula as the capitalization rate. The Capitalization Rate is commonly referred to as the Cap Rate. It helps brokers, investors and bankers evaluate an investment. It is used to compare one investment against another or others. The higher the cap rate the better for the investor.

Here is an example:

Income Side:

Let's say you want to calculate the value of a 3-family house.

The income is 3 apartments that are rented for $1,000 per month.

Therefore, the annual income is $36,000. We also refer to this as the Gross Income.

Apartment	Monthly	Annual
1	$1000	$12,000
2	$1000	$12,000
3	$1000	$12,000
Total	**$3000**	**$36,000**

Expense Side:

Let's say the following are the annual costs to operate the building:

Insurance:	$2,000
Real Estate Tax:	$6,000
Marketing:	$500
Legal:	$500
Accounting:	$500
Repairs:	$300
Electric:	$1,200
Total:	**$11,000**

Net Operating Income:

To calculate the Net Operating Income is easy:

The formula is Income minus Expenses equals NOI.

Income:	$36,000
Expenses:	$11,000
NOI:	**$25,000**

The Value

The last step is to take the NOI and divide it by the Cap Rate.

$$\frac{\$25,000}{.07} = \$357,143$$

The Replacement Philosophy

So, the value of this 3-family house is $357,143.

The Replacement Philosophy or Approach is very straightforward. It can be used for any type of real estate except for land.

The Replacement Philosophy is NOT to look at other things in the market; NOT to look at the subject property's metrics. This approach is to pretend there is a piece of vacant land next to the subject property.

You calculate what it would cost to buy the land and then design and build a duplicate building.

Let's go through an example in regard to a 10,000 square foot building on 1 acre of land:

In this method you need to contact an architect to give you an estimate on the cost to design the building. Usually, the architect will provide an estimate that will be a $/square foot cost. So, for example the architect may say the architect company charges $3.00/sf to design a building. If you have a 10,000 square foot building it could cost $30,000 to design.

Then you will need to ask a General Contractor for a "ball park" estimate on how much it will cost to build the building. Let's say his quote is $275 per square foot.

So, the cost to build the building will be $275,000.

Finally, how much does a similar piece of vacant land cost in that area. Let's say it is $25,000 per acre.

You then add up the three components:

Architect	$30,000
General Contractor	$275,000
Vacant Land	$25,000
Total	$330,000

In essence, it will cost $330,000 to make a duplicate or in other words a replacement.

It is imperative that a commercial real estate professional learn how to do all three of these methods.

Conducting Commercial Research

Conducting Research in regard to commercial real estate properties and commercial clients is both an art and a science.

Agents that are experts in residential real estate primarily use the **MLS**. Multiple Listing Service (**MLS**, also multiple listing system or multiple listings service. A multiple listing service's database and software is used by real estate brokers in real estate representing sellers under a listing contract to widely share information about properties with other brokers who may represent potential buyers or wish to work with a seller's broker in finding a buyer for the property or asset.

The **MLS** is a system that many residential real estate agents are forced into using. Normally, the real estate company pays a monthly fee for the agents to access the system. Then often the agents pay the company a monthly fee to access the **MLS**.

The **MLS** also has many rules that the users must abide by. For example, if you list your property in the **MLS** then all agents that are members of the **MLS** automatically become subagents of that property. All the members in the **MLS** can then legally represent the listing as a sub-agent.

In commercial real estate there are many databases that have information but the rules are different. Agents are not required to be part of the database and just because you have access to the database does NOT mean you have to co-broke with other agents.

In other words, if you subscribe to a commercial real estate database you basically are paying for the use of the data without any MLS rules.

A major difference between residential real estate information and residential real estate is that the vast majority of residential home sellers use a real estate agent. In 2018 87% of buyers purchased their home through a real estate agent or broker—a share that has steadily increased from 69 percent in 2001 (National Association of Realtors, 2018). Residential Home sales data is much more accurate than leasing statistics. The reason for this is that every municipality records house sales information so they can tax the home owner! So they try to be very accurate. Commercial lease info such as the rent that was agreed to is not recorded. A lot of data is conjecture.

In commercial real estate many buildings have their own in-house staff or market the building to be either leased or sold. The vast majority of buildings especially in urban areas have their own website so you can go on the building's website and see what office space or retail space is available. This service is free. Building Owners trying to lease space will never charge people to see their Space Available List. They want the world to know what spaces they have to rent and want people to contact them.

Other research that is important to commercial real estate professionals are:

- Absorption Rate Charts
- Board of Real Estate Reports
- Appraisal Companies Monthly Reports
- Occupancy Rate Charts
- New Building Permit Statistics
- Cap Rate Trends

In regard to finding commercial real estate prospects, smart commercial real estate pros will look at employment trends. For example, which companies are hiring more employees? Companies hiring more employees will need more space. If they need more space that means they need to sign a lease for additional space which results in another commission.

Another excellent way to find clients is by reading about mergers and acquisitions or commonly referred to as M and A deals. If two companies are merging that means that they will have duplicative departments. They will not need two accounting departments or two human resource departments, etc. As a result, the companies will need to dispose (sell) off some of their buildings.

Qualifying Businesses and Investors

Why do you want to qualify a prospect?

Avoid wasting <u>your</u> important time.
Avoid losing your money
Improve your efficiency
Increase your income faster
Avoid people using you
Educate and help the customer
Help you to prioritize

Why do brokers fail to qualify?

LAZINESS
Afraid to ask "sensitive" questions
Naïveté
Inexperienced
Greed takes over good business sense

The Irony of Qualifying

Real legitimate prospects want you to ask the "sensitive" questions
Real legitimate prospects understand the need to qualify them
Real legitimate prospects will respect you

Why do prospects refuse to be qualified?

They are lying
They want to use you and the company's resources for other purposes

They are not ready to be serviced
They need to be educated – help them
They don't have the authority to make the deal
They don't have the money

What type of prospects do you want to work with every day?

Prospects who have the true desire or need to do something
Prospects who have the money (now) to do something
Prospects who have the authority to do the deal

How do you only work with these types of prospects every day?

BY QUALIFYING <u>EVERYONE</u> YOU SPEAK WITH

Young Stock Broker Wasting Everyone's Time

This story is just one of many examples of how people can waste your time if they are not fully qualified.

One early morning a young stock broker perhaps 35 years old called me at the World Trade Center seeking to lease an office space in one of the Towers. He apologized for the short notice but needed to inspect the office space that afternoon. He was interested in a very specific office suite that was cited on our World Trade Center Space Available List.

I canceled a meeting I had planned and arranged for him to see the space right after lunch. He said he was bringing a few of his executives with him. Normally I would find out more about the prospect, that is, I would spend more time to qualify the prospect. But because of his "supposed" sense of urgency I was going to give the tour and then get the information later.

The young stock broker showed up with his entourage and wanted to go through the space quickly. I had an uncomfortable and suspicious feeling. While walking through the office space the prospect started talking about the space as though he ALREADY leased it. He was saying statements like; "This is our New York City office, this will be the reception area, here is our conference room..."

It then dawned on me that the people who were with him were not employees but POTENTIAL investors into his company. He was pretending that he already leased the space and was going to move in soon.

He was trying to scam the group of investors into thinking he already passed our creditworthiness test, negotiated the lease, paid a big security deposit, paid the first month's rent, etc.

I was not happy. So, I called him out and said "Since this is the first time you are seeing the space, do you think it will work for him. I will need financial statements soon."

Well my statement caused a stir and the investors were confused and then immediately became upset with the prospect.

The lesson learned was that you always need to qualify a prospect before you spend any substantive time with them.

Negotiating

The ability to negotiate deals very well is a critical skill that you must perfect if you want to be a highly successful commercial real estate expert.

I was very fortunate to have authored a critically acclaimed book on Negotiating entitled <u>Real Estate Dealmaking; A Property Investor's Guide to Negotiating</u>. If you want to hone your negotiating skills, I urge you to read this book.

Here is a short excerpt from the book:

Untrained negotiators always find themselves at a disadvantage. Just imagine trying to compete at an athletic game or a chess match without knowing how to play well. You put your short amount of training against a well-trained, experienced opponent. Of course, you al- ways can rely on the phenomenon of "beginner's luck." But do you really want to take a chance when it comes to negotiating details about such an important part of your life-the purchase of a home or an in- vestment property?

A highly trained negotiator understands the importance of having a plan that contains various alternatives, ready to be used to your advantage at a moment's notice. For example, if two investors were seeking to purchase the same property, the one who is a trained negotiator would have many basic advantages over an inexperienced negotiator. The trained negotiator would:

- Be able to determine the specific reason for the sale,
- have alternatives ready in a typewritten plan,
- know how to conduct research on all aspects of the negotiation,
- be prepared to overcome any objection or obstacle,
- be able to use other professionals appropriately,
- understand how to use flexibility as a strength,
- know how to prepare a priority list and sequence of negotiating topics,
- have strategies designed to meet deadlines in place, have the awareness to discern the weakness of the other side, and
- know when to use the technique of silence.

Negotiating is a skill that needs to be learned and practiced.

Time Management

The most important commodity of a commercial real estate agent in **time.**

Time management is the process of planning and exercising conscious control of the time spent on specific activities to work smarter than harder. It is a juggling act of various things that help you increase efficiency and strike a better work-life balance.

Improving your time management at work allows you to enhance your performance and achieve your desired goals with less effort and more effective strategies.

These are some steps that can help with time management:

1. Plan
2. Prioritize
3. Don't multitask
4. Get rid of distractions
5. Track your time
6. Schedule breaks
7. Find your most productive hours
8. Accept your limitations

(Kashyap, 2019)

Networking

Networking is an essential skill that needs to be honed if you are to become a successful commercial real estate professional.

Because you will be involved with clients from the business community, you need to get into the business community. There are so many great organizations that you can become part of. There are Chambers of Commerce, Trade Associations, Investment Clubs, etc. that you can join and perhaps eventually sit on their Boards.

Another benefit to becoming involved in these organizations is (if you like Public Speaking) to give a presentation to the group about commercial real estate in your area and how you can help businesses with any type of commercial real estate need they may have.

I had a great agent named Jay that worked for me that was an expert at networking. He went to as many events as he could physically endure. One month he went to 23 events! He was able to get many clients and truly became a known commercial real estate expert in the community.

Proposal Writing

When selling a house, the paperwork is less extensive than leasing an office or selling a strip mall.

Proposal writing is much more common in commercial real estate because you need to negotiate quite a few elements of the deal and then memorialize these items into the agreement each step of the way.

If you are managing quite a few deals at once, it is very helpful to have detailed proposals to keep track of all the deal components.

A very practical suggestion is to make a few key proposal templates that you can build upon once you begin to negotiate a particular transaction so you don't have to start from scratch with each new deal.

Chapter 4: Types of Clients

Types of Clients

Compared to potential residential clients, there are many more types of potential commercial clients you can work for. Basically, in residential real estate brokerage your clients are either buying or selling a home or they are renting an apartment. The types of commercial clients can be found in a very wide spectrum of industries. Every kind of business in the United States either rents a space or owns a building. One of the greatest pleasures in working in commercial real estate brokerage is that you can choose to work with an industry for which you have an affinity. If you are a "foodie" and like good and interesting restaurants you can choose to help restaurant owners find an ideal location, expand their premises, open a second place and/or sell their business. The following is a list of sub categories under the general term Commercial Real Estate. Keep in mind you can either focus in on one very particular type of clients or you can service a broad range of clients. Your real estate license permits you to do any type of real estate transactions.

Office Tenants

If you live near or within a metropolitan area take a look around at all of the office buildings. Every professional service company, for example lawyers, accountants, engineers, architects, web designers, etc. all need office space. They are all renting space and their leases do expire and they do need to either renew their lease or move to another location. In New York City there are estimated to be over 200,000 businesses (NYC.gov, n.d.). In Los Angeles there are 244,000 businesses. (LA County, n.d.), Dallas, Texas has almost 260,000 firms (QuickFacts, n.d.). The easiest and fastest way to make a living in commercial real estate is in office leasing when you represent the tenant. You can also work on the landlord side of an office building however, usually landlords want to hire someone with good experience. It is a rare occurrence that a landlord will hire a newbie to commercial real estate. The best way for a newbie to start on the landlord side of office leasing is to join a team as the "last man (or woman) on the totem pole.

Over the last 30 years I have negotiated thousands of leases. I also had the good fortune to manage one of the world's largest commercial real estate portfolios which included the World Trade Center in New York and many other office buildings, shopping centers, office parks and industrial parks. The portfolio consisted of over 20,000,000 square feet.

I have been involved with numerous real estate sales and lease negotiations with major firms such as Merrill Lynch, Bank of America, The Commodities Exchange, The Gap, JP Morgan Chase, Citibank, HSBC, The Bank of Tokyo, The Bank of Taiwan and thousands of other companies. I have also negotiated real estate deals with foreign governments including Japan, Russia and France.

Retail Tenants

Retail tenants come in all shapes and sizes. It is one of the most lucrative ways to make commercial real estate commissions. One of the most attractive aspects of being involved in retail leasing is if you like a particular consumer good, for example, fashionable shoes, trendy dresses, high tech gadgets, you can work on real estate deals related to your passion. You can represent an individual or a small company that is seeking to open their first boutique. Or you can represent a retail tenant that already has one or two locations and wants to expand their operation to a third, fourth and fifth location. Each time receiving a good commission for each location. Commercial customers come back to their real estate experts much more often than a typical home owner in the United States. According to the National Association of Realtors that the typical American family stay in their home for 9 years and increase of almost 50% since 2008. This means that a homeowner may use a broker to sell their home but then may not need them unto 10 years later! A very important part of being a retail leasing expert is that you need to understand demographics. Demographics are characteristics of a population. Characteristics such as race, ethnicity, gender, age, education, profession, occupation, income level, and marital status, are all typical examples of demographics.

Restaurants

Representing restaurants is an exciting profession. There are many, many types of restaurants you can work for. Take a look around any town or city in America. All of the places to eat, drink and be entertained in were found and transacted by a restaurant leasing expert. You can represent a small cozy restaurant, a café, a diner, a family restaurant, a fine-dining establishment, a franchise. The possibilities are truly endless. According to the National Restaurant Association, there were approximately 1,000,000 restaurants in the United States.

Warehouse Tenants

Working for a company that requires warehousing space is not glamourous however it is a very practical business and a much-needed part of many companies. There are also many types of warehouses. For example, some warehouses need a particular climate control, some need to be a "smart building", and others need to have the ability to drive a van or truck be able to drive right into the building. One important aspect of warehouse deals is that the size of the commission could be quite large. Warehouse buildings can be 100, 000 square feet, 200,000 square feet and even much greater than that. This equates to an opportunity to earn a large commission. Keep in mind the rental rates for a warehouse space are usually lower than an office space and lower than a retail space. A 100,000 square foot warehouse that can be leased for $10 per square foot per year equates to the tenant paying $1,000,000 in rent annually. If the lease is for 10 years the commercial real estate agent managing this deal could earn a commission that is approximately $320,000. Please see Chapter 9 on how commissions are paid to get a better understanding of the calculation.

Pop-Up Stores

A Pop-Up Store is a unique part of the commercial real estate brokerage business. A Pop-up is a situation where a retail store seeks to rent a space for a very short period of time. It could be as short as one or two months. The retailer usually takes over the space quickly and does not make any major changes to it. Technically, a lease is often not issued instead a permit or what is referred to as a license is granted to the retailer. The reason for this is that the landlord does not want the retailer to have strong rights of "temporary use of the space".

The worst situation for a landlord is when a retailer moves into a space and stops paying rent and then becomes a hold-over tenant. The landlord may have to spend a great deal of money on lawyer fees and spend a lot of time just to get the tenant out of the space. So, having the pop-up tenant sign a permit "signals' to everyone especially a judge in a court room that the intent was to give the tenant a very short-term use of the space. You need to act quickly to make good commissions if you are going to handle pop-ups. The reason is that the pop-up prospect usually does not give you enough lead time.

Pop-ups are often strategies used by companies to test a new idea or product. The companies can be very famous launching a new product line or they can be new startups that want to test the market before they go full speed ahead with renting a large store for a long period of time. Landlords like to rent out space to pop-ups when they have a space that is vacant waiting for a new tenant to move in.

A very good opportunity related to pop-ups is that you can easily make 2 commissions. The pop-up client usually will pay a commission, most often a set flat fee to find the ideal space. A landlord will also pay a commission. These deals are highly negotiable. Generally speaking, the fee from the landlord will be between 5% to 10% of the total aggregate rent. Let's look at a typical scenario: A well-known company is looking to launch a new product primarily to test the market. They are not opening the pop-up store to make a killing in profits. They are willing to spend $10,000 per month for a space that is 3,000 square feet. They need the space for 4 months. You have 60 days to find the space and lock in the deal. You find a landlord that has a space that is 3,000 square feet that another tenant will be taking the space in 6 months from now so the landlord cannot really lease the space for a long term but 4 months is possible. The pop-up tenant pays you a $5,000 fee for finding the space and negotiating the deal and the landlord pays you $4,000 ($40,000 x 10%) for bringing the landlord the tenant. The total fee is $9,000 for 2 months' worth of work. Typically, the permit to lease a pop-up store is only 2 or 3 pages long.

Investors

Working for investors is a tricky part of the commercial real estate business. It is what I refer to as the "the desire" side or "doesn't have to do" side of the business. This investor mentality can be very frustrating and it is often hard to read the investors' true intent. When an office leasing client's lease is expiring, they MUST renew their lease or move to a new space. An investor does not have that kind of motivation.

The worst experience for commercial real estate agents that handle investors is that they work for a client for months finding a good property, they start to negotiate a deal then the investor changes their mind and decides to invest in mutual funds, T-Bills, paintings, or classic cars, or simply keeps the money in the bank.

Over the many years of helping investors, I have found they fall into two different "camps". They are what I call either "Stock Players" or "Bond Players". It doesn't mean that they primarily buy stocks or buy bonds. I use these terms to define the risk mentality that the investor has. Are they risk oriented similar to the way a stock trader behaves or are they more risk adverse – similar to the way a person who invests in bonds behaves? Within the first five minutes of meeting an investor I will ask them "So in regard to real estate would you consider yourself similar to a stock trader who someone who invest in bonds?"

Builders Seeking Land

As a commercial real estate deal maker, you can work for builders, developers or contractors that routinely seek vacant land so that they can build their proposed properties. These particular clients are usually sophisticated and will want commercial real estate agents who have experience. To service these clients, you need to understand how they make money and the procedure it takes to get a piece of property approved.

Builders, developers and contractors have their own set of ratios that they use to determine if a piece of property is worthy for development. For example, let's say a builder is interested in building a few homes on the land that will be sold for $500,000. They may instruct you that they will only pay less than 25% of the $500,000 for each lot. To be more precise, if the builder can build 10 houses on the lot, the builder will only pay no more than $1,250,000 for the "dirt".

Also, a commercial real estate agent working for a builder needs to know how many "things" can be built onto the site. The key questions will be how many square feet of an office building can be built how many square feet of space that can be leased in a retail shopping strip, or how many warehouses, how many homes, etc. Some of the more particular skills you will need are an understanding of zoning, blueprint reading, basic construction procedures and costs. Often if the commercial real estate builder appreciates your abilities you may be able to make numerous commissions on one project. First, you will make the commission on the purchase of the land by the builder. Then after the project is built you may be given the assignment to lease out the space or sell the new building.

Doctors, Lawyers and Professional Services

There are thousands and thousands of doctors, lawyers and other professional service companies. According to Statista there were 1,340,000 lawyers in America in 2018. Some commercial real estate agents will choose one of these professional service industries and work that part of the market for their entire career. Professional services are most often financially sound and credit worthy. This is important to landlords.

Most professional service companies in urban areas will lease their space. Professional service companies in suburbia and rural communities will more often purchase their office space. Professional service companies are most concerned with the location of the property so that their patients or clients can visit them easily. Lawyers often prefer to be close to the courthouses. Doctors often like to be near hospitals. Architects and engineers like to be near the building department of the municipality. Most commercial real estate clients can be repeat customers however it is not as popular with clients such as doctors because once they establish themselves in a community they want to stay there for a very long time perhaps until they retire.

Manufacturers

Manufacturers are a unique breed in the world of commercial real estate clients

When you work for a manufacturing company execute looking to buy or sell a factory you need to be knowledgeable about the important aspects of the factory's physical space. For example, you need to understand what the floor load is in the building's various floors. Because it is important that the floor be able to withstand heavy loads such as fork lifts and other equipment. Floor loads are usually expressed in pounds per square foot.

The ceiling height is important to potential buyers because they may need to add equipment in the future that may be very tall.

How do you get raw materials and other materials into the manufacturing plant and how do you get the finished product out are key concerns?

Manufacturing plants especially the construction of a new facility sometimes gets caught up in a NIMBY situation. Nimby stands for Not In My Back Yard. In other words, the community may fight to be sure the factory does not get built because it usually decreases the value of nearby homes, causes congestion with trucks moving in and out, could cause noise and pollution. So, a commercial real estate agent needs to be mindful of what the community's position is on the transaction because they community can kill the deal and as a result, kill the commission.

Government Agencies

Obtaining a government agency as a client is not easy. Most of the time a government agency will hire a real estate agent to represent them through a process called RFPs: Request for Proposals. Quite simply, the government agency puts out an RFP either on-line and/or in the newspapers asking companies to review the RFP and answer all the questions and submit the information by a certain deadline. These RFPs are put out by the Federal Government, the State Government and the local governments.

Office Building Owners

Office Building Owners are some of the most sophisticated real estate professionals in the world. It is difficult for a new comer to commercial real estate to work solely and directly for an office building owner. They will insist that the real estate professionals who represent them have a deep understanding of commercial leasing and have a good track record of success.

When working for an office building owner you will need to maintain good relations with the existing tenants so that you can renew their leases and you will need to market the space to outside companies to attract them to the building and have them lease space.

Since you will handle all the renewals in the building you are pretty much guaranteed a steady stream of commissions. In addition to receiving a commission on a lease renewal, you will also receive commission regarding existing tenants if they expand their leasehold.

For a small office building, for example, a building with 20 tenants or less can probably be handed by one commercial agent. For larger office buildings, the building owner may want a team of commercial real estate professionals to handle the marketing and the leasing.

One important aspect of being an office building rep is that you will probably have an office in the building and stay in the building each day. Prospective tenants will come to you.

Strip Mall Owners

The owners of strip malls are excellent clients to work for. Similar to Office Building Owners they are usually look for an experienced commercial real estate professional or team of professionals.

The primary goal of representing a particular strip mall is to fill it up quickly and keep it full at 100% occupancy. Having a vacant store in a strip mall really reduces the appeal of the strip mall. In an office building the general public is not aware if a building, for example, has 10 vacant office spaces.

If you represent a strip mall you will also be paid a commission if the existing tenant renews their lease. But you need to be mindful that the leases in a strip mall are often long-term such as 15 years. So, you may have to wait 15 years to get another commission from a particular tenant transaction.

You will need to know more variations on how the rent can be paid to the owner. For example, some retail tenants will pay a percentage rent, some will pay a base rent and some will pay a combination.

More than likely, you will not have an office in the strip mall. You will work for a separate location because to have you occupy space in the strip mall is not cost-effective for the strip mall owner. They want to lease every single square inch to retailers so they can maximize their rental income.

Landowners Seeking a Buyer

Representing a landowner seeking a buyer is a bit more difficult in regard to finding the right buyer.

When you represent an office building there are many tenants you can solicit because so many companies lease office space. Trying to find someone to buy a specific amount of acreage is not easy.

In addition, land does not usually increase dramatically in a short period of time unless it is smack in the path of development.

Because of the slow increase in its value, landowners sometime become impatient and want unreasonable amounts of money for their land especially if it is unimproved.

One thing to keep in mind with landowners is that they rarely have land that is generating revenue. Some do, for example, if they allow a timber company to extract trees.

It is one of the areas of commercial real estate where you really need to be up to speed on zoning. For example, if you represent a large piece of residential land you need to know how many houses can be built on the site, how much acreage is needed for roadways, buffer zones, frontage, and etc.

One general rule of thumb is 20% for roadways and access.

Big Company versus Small Company

Where to work is important to your success. It is possible to conduct commercial real estate transactions while you are in your residential company. There are some positive aspects to this and some drawbacks.

If the residential real estate company you are presently working in does not have a commercial real estate division it may not be considered a serious company to a potential commercial real estate client. In other words, if you hand your business card to an executive of a company or the owner of a business and the name of your company exudes residential real estate, quaint homes, wonderful apartments, etc. you will not be taken seriously. It will appear as though you are conducting a "side job".

On the other hand, if your company does not have a commercial real estate division and you have an interest in generating more money for yourself and your company, it may be a good time to start a new division called; Commercial Real Estate.

I have helped many people start their commercial real estate businesses and I always enjoy providing consulting services to companies that have a new found passion to start a new commercial real estate department or section of their company.

If it is not possible to become a commercial real estate agent in your company because it will seem awkward to potential clients or your company is not yet ready to truly create a commercial real estate company. You may need to move to another company. One of the important decisions that a residential agent needs to consider is whether to work for a big company with many agents and offices or work for a smaller firm.

Big Company: Pros and Cons

Big commercial real estate companies are powerful enterprises with enormous influence in the market. There is a great amount of opportunity within the company but its sheer size can devour you.

Here are the positives and negatives of working in a large organization:

Negative Aspects:

No Access to the Boss -When you work at a major, large company it is rare that the new agent will get to spend quality time with the President or Chairman of the company. In some cases, the agent may never even get to meet the top executives.

You're Put in a Silo – Many big companies do not want you to be "roaming" from one group to another so they will put you on a select team. That team, for example, may only work on office deals and nothing else. Big companies need more conformity so they try to keep you focused on one area of the commercial industry – they keep you in the silo.

Less Commissions – It is rare for a new company to have a newbie start working on his or her own deals. You are usually put on a team. Since you will be the "low person on the totem pole" you will get a smaller percentage of the commission.

Also, if a company has to pay a franchise fee to the franchisor (HQ) then your commission will be reduced by say 6%; because the company has to pay a royalty on every transaction.

More Rules – In a large organization there will be more rules, more Standard Operating Procedures (SOPs). They do not want people to "disrupt" the procedures that are put in place.

One of many – Because some organizations may have 30, 50, 100 or more real estate professionals on staff, you may get lost in the crowd. It is often hard for managers and mentors to spend a lot of quality time with you if you are simply one of many.

Client Restrictions – The major players in commercial real estate represent both landlords and tenants. This sets the situation for conflicts of interest. Even though there is supposed to be a "firewall" between the Tenant Rep Agents and the Landlord Agents it really isn't a wall but more of a fuzzy line. Quite often upper management will tell the Tenant Agents to make sure their clients visit the buildings they represent and to limit the clients' exposure to other buildings – which in fact maybe very suitable for the client.

General Training – Many large companies have general training that you may be required to attend. There is merit to this education but more personalized training may be something you prefer or will find more worthwhile.

Positive Aspects

Brand Awareness – Probably the best part of being in a big company is that they have brand awareness. People recognize the name so you can have instant credibility if the company has a good reputation

History – Usually big companies have been around for a while and many clients like the idea that the company had longevity.

Referrals – Because big companies may have many offices, they often will send referrals to your particular office. So, for example if a company in California needs to lease space in New York they will send you a referral. The down side is that you may have to pay that California office up to 35% of the gross commission because they gave you the lead.

Many People to Ask – Since these big companies have many agents there will be more people around to ask questions or ask for solutions to problems. Large companies do foster competition, so it is important that the big company have a culture where agents do honestly help one another and not stab each other in the back.

Small to Mid-Sized Company: Pros and Cons

Positive Aspects

Working for a small company instead of a big company has many benefits. I characterize a small company as a firm that has approximately 20 agents or less. Here are a few of the main points:

Access to the Boss – As a beginner in commercial real estate it is important that you have a mentor. The owner or broker-of-record is usually a competent, experienced commercial real estate professional. A great benefit to working for a small company is that you will have easy access to the owner.

See Everything – Working in a small company will give you exposure to see many types of deals. Seeing all the deals that are going on in an office is a great form of education.

Personal Attention – Because the company is small there is more of a sense of a "tight-knit" group and there is more likelihood that you will receive more personal attention.

Easier to Become a Partner – In a large company the environment is much more competitive and many more people may vie to become a partner. In a smaller company, the odds may be easier to become a partner if you do well and have the appropriate traits and track record to become a partner.

Less Rules – Large companies need to have more rules because they need to have more order when managing a very large group of agents. However, in a smaller firm there may be some basic rules but ownership is more approachable to changing the rules or go around the rules.

More Nimble – A smaller company is usually faster to change to market conditions and to new technology. A large company is like a big ocean liner. It is dependable and has power but to turn a big ship or to get it to speed up quickly is difficult. A small company is like a good speedboat – very easy to change course and to accelerate. So, if a new technology comes out that may help the agents, an owner of a small company can literally decide to acquire it overnight. A large company may have to go through a process or a committee or a budget review first, etc.

Focused Training – In a large company that has many, many agents it is very difficult to give one-on-one in-person training to everyone. It is more efficient for big companies to do large mass training or training on line which is good. However, personal one-on-one training is always best.

Negative Aspects

Brand Name – A small company may not have the national reputation. It may only have a local reputation which still can be beneficial.

Longevity – Age highly successful company may be able to withstand changes in the market cycle. A smaller company may not be able to withstand a bad downturn and could cause the company to fold.

Which one to choose?

I am often asked which company is best to choose when first starting out in commercial real estate. I always advise people who are contemplating a profession in commercial real estate that they should work for a small company first because there will be more benefits to them to hone their skill.

I believe once you gain some experience "under your belt" you can try and work for a larger firm.

Chapter 5: What Kind of Properties

What kind of properties do you want to work with? The list below show some of the different types. What are you interested in? What do you already have knowledge in? What would you like to learn more about? What is your niche?

1. Medical, Pharmacy and Veterinary- There are lot of medical properties from hospitals to medical corridors, right down to individual doctor, dentist offices, and veterinary offices. There is also medial manufacturing that has very specific requirements.

2. Night clubs- Night clubs have areas all their own, there may be zoning and licensing restrictions on the location of clubs.

3. Sports- You could be brokering deals for a new arena, indoor soccer fields, or even golf courses.

4. Office Buildings- Office Buildings can be filled with lawyers, accountants, or many various others that need space for people, computers and clients.

5. Warehouses and Distribution Centers- These spaces can be large and open and may be situated near transportation hubs to facilitate stock movement and have lots of square footage but the price per square foot is less but the deals can still be very lucrative.

6. Dispensaries- This is a new area that may be complicated by local zoning and local law, knowledge of this would be necessary. .

7. Hotels- These can be large structures that have some aspects that overlap other areas, as they may be near transportation, require large space but also need to be near population, workplaces or attractions.

8. Resorts and Amusement Parks-These may start as large tracts of lands and will probably need significant knowledge of zoning and working with the planning board.

9. Farms and Ranches- Farms are a commodity in this country and if you are brokering a deal from one farmer to another or to a large farming company you need to have knowledge of the needs for that type of farm or ranch, beef cattle have very different needs than dairy cattle or the needs of corn or wheat.

10. Strip Malls- If the strip mall has already been built you may be leasing out the individual spaces or you may work on the planning for the actual construction of the strip mall.

11. Shopping centers- Like strip malls, shopping centers can be built or already constructed, these big structures may have variety of uses from supermarkets down to mom and pop shops, they can be one building or a huge exterior mall.

12. Not for profits—these can be interesting to work for and they have a clear mission, this determines the area and uses, and can overlap with many of the properties listed above.

Chapter 6: The Many Types of Commercial Real Estate Jobs

Another great aspect of the commercial part of the real estate industry is that there are many different types of jobs related to commercial real estate. Here are a few:

Commercial Real Estate Agent (Salesperson) – This is the first step in a real estate brokerage company. You need to study in a State-approved school and take a State exam to become licensed as a real estate agent. In regard to licensing laws there is no such thing as a "commercial license" or "residential license". Once you receive a real estate license you can practice any kind of real estate. A real estate agent or salesperson will most likely be on commission.

Commercial Real Estate Broker – This is the highest position in a real estate brokerage company. By law, you start out as a Commercial Real Estate Salesperson (Agent). The Broker is someone who has worked for a number of years as a Real Estate Salesperson (each State in the United States has its own rules about how to "graduate" from Salesperson to Broker. This is most often a commission only position.

Commercial Office Leasing Manager – This position is the person who is in charge of the leasing of a particular building or sometimes a portfolio of office buildings. If the Commercial Office Leasing Manager only works for one company at one building, he usually does not have to be licensed. If the building is not too large the Commercial Office Leasing Manager may be able to handle all duties in regard to leasing up the office building. A Commercial Office Leasing Manager usually has his office in the building he is leasing up. The position is most often a salaried position with fringe benefits. Sometimes there may be a bonuses part of the compensation package.

Commercial Retail Leasing Manager – This position is also usually a salaried position similar to the Commercial office Leasing Manager position cited above. The only difference is that this professional will manage the leasing of a retail property such as a shopping mall.

Site Selection Manager or Director – A Site Selection Manager or Director is someone whose primary responsibilities are finding the new locations for a company then negotiating the leases. For example, Starbucks may have an employee who goes and scouts out new locations for the company to install a new coffee shop. This position is usually a salaried position with fringe benefits. Quite often, extensive travel is required.

Head of Global Real Estate – The Head of Global Real Estate or a similar title is usually a very high-level person in a large company. The position's responsibilities are very broad and very important.

Usually the Head of Global Real Estate will be responsible for the leasing, buying and selling of all real estate throughout the world. This could include a portfolio consisting of office space, retail stores, warehouses, manufacturing plants, datacenters, distribution facilities, etc. The position may be responsible for all aspects of the portfolio which could include but not be limited to leasing, property management, design and construction, remodeling, furnishings and security. This are very high paying salaried jobs with fringe benefits. People selected to fill these positions have very deep experience.

Asset Manager – The Asset Manager position's main responsibility is to manage the asset. There is no one set of responsibilities. Each building's owners will prescribe what responsibilities the Asset Manager will watch over. The key goal of the Asset Manager is to optimize the value of the property or the portfolio. To do this they are involved with important aspects such as risk management, working with lenders especially in regard to refinancing situations, making efficient use of capital, overseeing the property manager and continually determining the value of the property and finding ways to improve its value.

Commercial Real Estate Analyst – The position of a Commercial Real Estate Analyst is more of a behind-the-scenes position. It is considered a support position. The primary responsibilities of a Commercial Real Estate Analyst are to gather

information about a particular building or portfolio
and calculate different scenarios to help sellers or
buyers in their investment decision-making. The
Commercial Real Estate Analyst must be very adept
at using various software to help run calculations to
determine value or create an asset management plan.
The position is a salaried position often including
fringe benefits.

Chapter 7: How Long is the Sales Cycle?

An important question that people who are contemplating a career in commercial real estate often ask is:

> "How long will it take me to close a deal?"

The answer depends on two aspects of the commercial real estate transaction. The determining factors are what type of transaction and the size of the deal.

Office Lease Deals

Relatively speaking, the fastest transaction to make a commission in commercial real estate is an office leasing deal. The reason is twofold:

> An office lease tenant does not have as many concerns or considerations as a retail lease deal or an industrial leasing deal. Retail tenants need to know about the demographics of an area, where the competition is, how much frontage, how do people enter the parking lot, etc. These considerations are time-consuming for the commercial real estate agent. The office tenant often doesn't care if there are other similar business in the building. Office tenants usually are not concerned with demographics.

The second aspect is the size of the transaction. For example, if a company only has 20 employees, they may need about 5,000 square feet. A company can move 20 employees over a weekend. So, the transaction can move quickly.

If a company has 100 employees, they may need 25,000 square feet. Relocating 100 employees takes much more logistical planning and will take longer.

A typical office leasing deal for a small company such as the 20-person company cited above should – from A to Z - take less than 90 days. A to Z means from the day you meet the client it should take 1 month to understand their needs and conduct research, it should take the next month to go out and look at space and choose the best office space, the final month should be dedicated to writing the proposal and getting the actual lease finalized and signed.

Retail Lease Deals

The second fastest way to make a commercial real estate commission is to represent a retail tenant in a retail lease deal. As mentioned above the retail client will have more things to consider before they lease the space.

The research and touring of spaces will take longer. This phase could take 1 to 3 months. There are usually more components in a retail lease. For example, some items that need to be negotiated are signage, exclusivity, a kick-out clause, a Good Guy clause, the right to audit, etc. These clauses are normally not in an office lease. Therefore, this phase of the process may take longer. Perhaps 1 to 2 months.

One specific time sensitive element that may drive the deal to be done faster is that quite often a retailer wants to be into their new space in September or October so they can prep up for the holiday season and capture all that great revenue.

Investor Deals

The type of commercial real estate deal that can take longer is what I call a "desire" deal. An investment is not a "must do" kind of deal. When an office tenant needs to find a space because his existing lease is ending and the Landlord said they are not renewing them, this is called a "must do" scenario. The deal must get done or the company will have no place to operate their business!

An investor especially one that has high standards and very particular economic metrics (for example, a specific Cap Rate, a specific GRM, a specific Cash – on – Cash return) may take a long time to make a decision.

An investor could take 6 months to 1 year just to make the decision to enter into a Contract of Sale. The worse part of dealing with an investor is that they may have you work for 1 year and then decide not to invest in real estate but change their mind and invest in stocks, bonds, art work, classic cars, etc.

Chapter 8: Making Money in Business Brokerage

Business Brokerage

Another exciting, very lucrative part of being a commercial real estate agent is the off-shoot profession of business brokerage.

Every year in America over 500,000 businesses are bought and sold. And someone is making a lot of commissions on those transactions.

Business brokerage is the livelihood of representing buyers and sellers of businesses. Think of any kind of business and most likely there was someone there to broker the deal.

The reason you need a real estate license to be involved with business brokerage is that the vast majority of the time there is real estate involved with the sale whether it is a commercial real estate lease that comes along with the purchase of the business or perhaps a physical asset such as a building, or store, warehouse, land, etc.

A key skill required to be good at business brokerage is the ability to value a business. Similar to a large commercial real estate deal there are many parts to a business. For example; when someone buys a business, here is a very small sample of what they may be acquiring:

- A building or a lease
- Inventory
- Equipment
- Customer database
- The Brand Names
- Existing employees
- The methods and procedures
- Intellectual Property

Each of these important items need to be examined and negotiated into the deal.

The commission to help someone sell their business is usually 10% of the total value of the deal.

I cite the word "value" because a smart commercial real estate broker has to be cautious about how to word their commission agreement. Someone may buy a business but instead of an all cash-deal maybe the owner will "hold paper" that is they will hold a note so the buyer is paying them payments over time. There may be a stock swap, the seller may still hold a minority interest in the company, etc.

So, the broker needs to be sure he or she is paid based on the whole value of the deal.

Another important characteristic a commercial broker involved in business brokerage must have is a great sense of discretion. It sounds antithetical. Someone asks you to try very hard to sell their business but they don't want you to let the public know the place is for sale. A classic case is where a restaurant owner does not want the broker to put a for sale sign outside the restaurant. The owner does not want ads placed in the paper or on-line where the actual name is cited.

Why?

Because once people know the place is for sale the business may start to dwindle; people may think the business is not good that is why they are selling and most importantly this devalues the price and a potential buyer will try to squeeze the seller for a much lower price.

You also need to be a "quick study" type of person. You need to quickly inspect the business, observe how they make money, watch their procedures and processes, because you will need to explain these elements to a potential buyer.

The paperwork can be a bit less than say a typical retail lease deal because the paperwork is basically a term sheet, an inventory sheet, and then the lease or deed can roll up into the deal. The lease does not have to be negotiated because the new owner is simply taking over the lease. Technically, it is called a Lease Assignment.

Another legal item that is very rarely seen in a residential deal is an NDA. NDA stands for Non-Disclosure Agreement. It is often requested by the seller that the broker AND the buyer sign an NDA stating they will not disclose any information given to them to any other person.

Why?

Because if the information about their revenue, their profits, their "secret sauce", etc. fell into their competitor's hands it could do irreparable harm to their business.

In my 30 plus years of working with business owners I have never met a business owner who thought the professional evaluation conducted by myself (or other analysts, or other appraisers, etc.) was an accurate valuation.

Business owners ALWAYS think their business is worth a lot more than what the cold hard facts of the analysis state.

Why?

Because many times the owner put his heart and soul into growing the business, spent years sweating and toiling, deeply committed 24 hours – 7 days per week to build the business, spent numerous hours away from his or her family. So, because of how human nature is, the seller always overestimates what the value of the business is worth.

Business brokerage is a great business to be involved in. If you have an inkling that it might be right for you, I urge you find a mentor, learn the ropes and give it a try.

Chapter 9: Getting Paid

Some of the most frequently asked questions about operating in the world of commercial real estate are "How do I get paid?" "Who pays me?" and "How is the commission calculated?".

Generally speaking, commercial real estate agents make more income than residential agents. There are quite a number of reasons for this. The income has to do with the particular type of deal, the industry standard for commercial commissions, the size of the deal and sometimes it'll it to obtain two commissions on one deal.

And residential real estate brokerage usually there is a 6% commission. This is not a law or something mandatory. It is simply a common standard. A 6% is a function of the market. Many companies have tried to do deals for a lot less, for example a 2% commission. Many companies have tried to always obtaining much higher commission say 10%. The vast majority of the time they fail. The failure is a simple factor of the market.

Let's review why this 6% seems to work the best in residential real estate brokerage. The 6% commission is usually paid by the person or persons selling their home. The 6% commission is paid to the company who was given the assignment to sell the home.

That company who receives the 6% commission will then usually split the 6% with the real estate brokerage company that was given the assignment by the buyer to find a home. In essence, the seller's brokerage company and the buyer's brokerage company each receive a 3% commission.

The companies then give a portion of the commission to the specific sales agent.

So, for example if you are an average agent you may receive half of the 3% commission that the real estate brokerage company received.

It is important to note that the way the real estate brokerage commission payment works is that the real estate company that represents the seller pays the other real estate company and then the respective companies to pay the individual agents that worked on the deal. Homeowners are not allowed to pay a real estate agent directly. They must pay the real estate brokerage company.

So here is an example of a typical real estate commission split for a residential home in the United States:

A $300,000 home was sold from the Smith Family to the Jones Family.

Mary Jackson is an agent that works for the ABC Real Estate Company and was the *Seller's real estate agent.* The Smith Family agreed to pay the ABC Real Estate Company 6%.

Joe Gordon is an agent that works for XYZ Real Estate Company and was the *Buyer's real estate agent.*

ABC Real Estate Company agrees to split their commission with XYZ Real Estate Company.

The Smith Family pays ABC Real Estate Company $18,000.   ($300,000 x 6% = $18,000)

ABC Real Estate Company sends $9,000 (half their commission) to XYZ Real Estate Company.

ABC Real Estate Company pays 60% of their commission to Mary ($9,000 x 60% = $5,400)

XYZ Real Estate Company pays 50% of their commission to Joe ($9,000 x 50% = $4,500)

Final Results:

ABC Real Estate Company: $3,600

Mary Jackson: $5,400

XYZ Real Estate Company: $4,500

Joe Gordon $4,500

Total $18,000

If the agents involved in the sale of his home spent three months getting the transaction done, Mary would have made $1,800 per month and Joe would have made $1,500 per month.

$300,000 Home with 6% Commission

Seller's Agent's Company $300,000 at 6% =**$18,000**

50% of $18,000 goes to each company = **$9,000 per company**

3 months for sale	Seller's Agent	Seller's Company		**Seller's Company**
Per month income	60%	40%		
$1,800	$5,400	$3,600	$9,000	
	Buyer's Agent	Buyer's Company		**Buyer's Company**
Per month income	50%	50%		
$1,500	$4,500	$4,500	$9,000	

To make a good living in the United States, residential real estate agents need to sell more than 1 deal per month.

Keep in mind the real estate company in the above example must take their share of their commission, for example in the case of the $3,600 that the ABC Real Estate Company received and take that income and pay many bills to run the company. Those bills may include:

- Office Rent
- Electricity
- Insurance
- Real Estate Tax
- HVAC expenses
- Advertising
- Website Development and Management
- Brochures, flyers, etc.
- Signage

Now if a real estate company advertises and promises to carry out a professional assignment for 2% then all of the parties cited above in the example would receive one-third less for that particular deal or in other words the money that would be received would look like:

Final Results with only a 2% Commission:

ABC Real Estate Company: $1,200

Mary Jackson: $1,800

XYZ Real Estate Company: $1,500

Joe Gordon $1,500

Total $9,000

So, Mary would have worked for $600 for the month.

Joe would have worked for $500 for the month.

They would have to do a lot more deals to make a decent living.

$300,000 Home with 2% Commission

Seller's Agent's Company $300,000 at 2% =**$6,000**

50% of $6,000 goes to each company **= $3,000 per company**

3 months for sale	Seller's Agent	Seller's Company		Seller's Company
Per month income	60%	40%		
$600	$1,800	$1,200	$3,000	
	Buyer's Agent	Buyer's Company		Buyer's Company
Per month income	50%	50%		
$500	$1,500	$1,500	$3,000	

In regard to the other extreme where some residential companies have tried to obtain 10% commission from homeowners, it is a very rare occurrence because 10% cuts too deep into the money that the homeowner receives from a sale. Very often when homeowners sell their houses, they have to pay off a mortgage and may be left with a small or medium-sized profit. They also may have to pay a lawyer and have other expenses related to preparing the house for a sale.

So, the 10% would be a percentage of the gross amount the homeowner receives not 10% of the profit the homeowners receive. So here is an example where a homeowner may be unhappy with the way the money is divided.

If a homeowner sells a house for $300,000 and has a mortgage of $200,000 the division of the $100,000 in profit may be divided as follows:

Real Estate agents receives $30,000 ($300,000 x 10% = $30,000)

Lawyer received $2,000

Money towards other expenses to prepare the house for sale: $2,000

The Homeowner is left with $66,000

$300,000 Home with 10% Commission

$300,000 for House	
Brokers' Fees	$30,000
Lawyer's Fees	$2,000
Expenses to prepare house for sale	$2,000
Mortgage	$200,000
Total Expenses	**$234,000**
Home Owner Profit	**$66,000**

Also, when real estate agents try to go too high with their demand for a 10% or 9% or 8% commission, there will always be another company out there willing to go down. The catch is other real estate companies will go down in their requests but they usually will not want to go below 6% for the reasons stated above.

Now let's examine how commissions are calculated in commercial real estate.

The basic logic used in commercial real estate is that the deal maker (the commercial real estate agent) should get a percentage of the lease rent and/or the sales price of the property.

Commercial Real Estate agents can be paid commissions in five primary ways:

1. The commercial real estate agent receives a percentage of the projected rent from a tenant's lease.

2. The commercial real estate agent receives a percentage of the sale of a building. This is similar to a residential agent selling a home.

3. The commercial real estate agent can receive 2 commissions; one from the sale of the building and then a commission from a lease. This occurs in sales-leaseback transactions which will be explained in this chapter.

4. The commercial real estate agent can be paid a percentage of the sale of a business. This is commonly referred to as business brokerage. People who concentrate on the sale of businesses need a real estate license because the vast majority of business sales include the transfer of property such as an office building, a warehouse, a store, etc. The transfer could be the sale of the real estate or the transfer of a lease.

5. The commercial real estate agent can get paid by doing a BOV (a Broker's Opinion of Value). This is usually a set fee. In residential real estate it is unusual to be paid a fee to calculate the value of a home. In commercial real estate it is common to be paid a separate fee to calculate the value of a property or the value of a lease.

Leasing

The logic applied in commercial leasing is that the commercial real estate agent should receive a percentage of the overall rent. So, if the lease is for 15 years the commission will be much greater than a lease that is 10 year long and much greater than a lease that is only 5 years. It is important to note that the amount of effort exerted by a commercial real estate agent for these cited leases (i.e. a 5-year lease, a 10-year lease, a 15-year lease) is all the same.

There are 2 primary ways a landlord or building owner will calculate a commission to a commercial real estate agent:

The New York Method

The landlord establishes what is referred to as a Commission Schedule. The word Schedule has nothing to do with calendars or scheduling it is actually just a list of calculations. Also see the section on Typical Documents

It looks something like this:

OFFICE LEASES

On the rental for all or any fraction of:

The First and Second Years:	5%
The Third Year:	4%
The Fourth, Fifth, Sixth, and Seventh Years:	3%
The Eighth, Ninth, and Tenth Years:	2.5%
The Eleventh Year and Beyond:	2%

RETAIL LEASES

On the rental for all or any fraction of:

The First Year:	6%
The Second Year:	5%
The Third, Fourth, and Fifth Years:	4%
The Sixth, Seventh, Eighth, Ninth, and Tenth Years:	3%
The Eleventh Year through the Twentieth Year:	2%
The Twenty-First Year and Beyond	1%

The landlord calculates the total commission using this schedule. It does NOT reflect the number of times you get paid. Many real estate agents get confused when they see this because they think they receive a commission each year and they have to wait years to be paid. This is not true.

Some landlords pay the entire amount when the lease is signed. I believe the best way for the payment of the commission to be made is:

50% of the commission when the lease is fully signed by both parties.

50% of the commission when the tenant moves in.

Here is a typical example of how a commercial real estate agent gets paid on an office lease:

The following example would be considered a small deal. Let's say the client is an engineering firm with 20 employees and the commercial real estate agent successfully finds an office space and negotiates a good lease for the engineering firm. A good rule of thumb to calculate the needs of an office tenant is 250 square feet per person. This does not mean each person gets an office of 250 square feet. For a company with 20 people you need a reception area, a conference room, a kitchenette etc. The 250 square feet per person takes all this into account.

So, the office space is 5,000 square feet.

Let's say the rent is $25 per square foot and the rent increase 3% per year. (Note: Dollar per square foot is defined by dollar per square foot per year) The frst year's rent will be $125,000.

The commission would be as follows:

5000 sq. ft. at $25/sq. ft. with 3% increase per year

Year 1	$125,000.00	5.0%	$6,250.00
Year 2	$128,750.00	4.0%	$5,150.00
Year 3	$132,612.50	3.0%	$3,978.38
Year 4	$136,590.88	3.0%	$4,097.73
Year 5	$140,688.60	3.0%	$4,220.66
Year 6	$144,909.26	3.0%	$4,347.28
Year 7	$149,256.54	3.0%	$4,477.70
Year 8	$153,734.23	2.5%	$3,843.36
Year 9	$158,346.26	2.5%	$3,958.66
Year 10	$163,096.65	2.5%	$4,077.42
	$1,432,984.91		$44,401.16

The Commercial real estate brokerage company receives two checks:

$22,200.58 on the day of the lease signing

$22,200.58 when the tenant moves into their space

As you can see this commission calculation is hard to do off the top of your head so many commercial real estate agents use this Rule of Thumb:

A 5-year lease deal will have a total commission approximately 20% of the first year's annual rent.

A 10-year lease deal will have a total commission approximately 32% of the first year's annual rent.

A 15-year lease deal will have a total commission approximately 42% of the first year's annual rent.

So, to use the rule of thumb in the example we stated above you would calculate the commission as follows:

It is a 10-year lease so the commission will be 32% of $125,000 which equals $40,000.

Pretty close.

The New Jersey Method

In some parts of the United States commercial lease commissions are calculated in a more straightforward method. I refer to this methodology as the New Jersey Method.

Basically, the calculation is made by taking a single % and multiplying the aggregate total rental income of the lease.

Usually the percentage is 3%. Here is how the commission is calculated in regard to the example cited above.

The total rent from all 10 years is equal to $ $1,432,984.91. You then multiply this by 3% and the total commission is $ $42,989.55

.

Chapter 10: How to Find Clients

The most important commodity a real estate professional has is **time.**

Whether you are a residential real estate agent or a commercial real estate agent the one thing you cannot waste is time. It is critical that you know how to determine prospects from suspects. Great marketing campaigns must be comprehensive. To rely on just one way to market to potential clients is risky. The following are the best methods to attract commercial real estate clients. You should become adept at all of them.

The Efficiency and Effectiveness of Email Campaigns

Before there were laptops and smart phones, before there was the ability to email messages commercial real estate professionals still made a great deal of money. They did it by sending letters typed on a type writer and sent through the United States Post Office. The ability to email has led the way for commercial real estate agents to supercharge their ability to reach out to prospects.

Business people communicate by email every day so it is not considered intrusive if your email is done professionally and courteously. The most important element to a good email is that it "gives" the reader something. Too many people "ask for something" in their emails.

Referrals May Be the Best and Primary Source for Clients

Most marketing tactics are referred to as "Cold" solicitation. The classic example is cold calling which means that the person you are calling does not have a warm relationship with you. You are calling them "out of the blue". It is always better to contact people that you may know already or if they are introduced to you by a mutual friend.

Networking Events – the Clients Are standing in Front of You

Networking is a very important aspect of finding clients. One of the differences between residential and commercial real estate networking is that there are many business venues to discuss business related subjects and at these venues the attendees expect you to talk about your business. They will not be offended if you bring it up. At some business networking events they encourage you to solicit other people at the event.

In regard to residential brokerage you need to be a bit more discerning about when and how to solicit people. For example, at a business event it may appear to be intrusive to an executive if you start asking them with, they live, would they be interested in selling their home, etc.

At business events there is a lot of "selling" going on. People anticipate it and enjoy it.

In residential brokerage residential real estate agents often try to network at birthday parties, holiday parties, weddings, etc. Some people may be turned off by that and may not want you to be out at the event "selling" yourself.

A critical, realistic thought to networking is why you are there. The goal is not to sell something directly at that moment. You may be lucky and someone may be particularly interested and may want to get right down to negotiating that evening. But the likelihood is very slim. The true goal at a networking event is to get your prospect to accept a meeting from you.

Networking is an initial step in the "Selling Sequence". Basically, you meet a prospect. You try your best to make a good first impression without going overboard. Convince the prospect that you can help them and ask them professionally and politely if you can follow up about getting together so you can explain in more detail specifically how you can help them.

The idea is that you should come across as OFFERING or GIVING something not that you are ASKING for something. There is a big difference between these two perceptions.

In regard to networking you need to do 5 important things before each business event to make the networking most productive.

1. Practice your 1-minute elevator speech. An elevator speech is elevator speech is a short description of an idea, product or company that explains the concept in a way such that any listener can understand it in a short period of time. This description typically explains an individual person, the description generally explains one's skills and goals, and why they would be a productive and beneficial person to have on a team or within a company or project. An elevator pitch can be used to entice an investor or executive in a company, or explain an idea. The goal is simply to convey the overall concept or topic in an exciting way. Unlike a sales pitch, there may not be a clear buyer–seller relationship. The name—elevator pitch—reflects the idea that it should be possible to deliver the summary in the time span of an elevator ride, or approximately thirty seconds to two minutes.

2. Bring a lot of cards with you and be determined to hand them all out.

3. Review the attendees list to see who you definitely should meet at the event.

4. Call the host and ask them if they could be so kind to introduce you to the "must see" people at the event. Having the host

introduce you validates you and is a very efficient way to meet the prospects.

5. BEFORE the event prepare an email or letter that will be ready to go out to each person you met at the event. This way as soon as you get back to your home or office you can easily and quickly just add their name and other contact info to the email or letter and send it out. The prospect will more likely remember you and agree to meeting with you.

Letters Are Still Impressive

When was the last time you received a professional letter, personally sent to you and actually signed by the sender? With the advent of email, it was probably a long time ago. You probably don't get that many.

There is something good to be said about taking the time to send a personal letter through the mail to the prospect especially if the letter is well written and looks very crisp, and professional.

It says something about your sincere intention, your professionalism and your focus. Recipients get so many emails nowadays that an authentically signed letter gets a lot of attention.

Another reality all business people must face is that there are very strong, impenetrable "sentinels" that guard executives. These sentinels prevent emails getting to their boss. Some executives have all their emails routed to their secretary or assistant first before they see it. Many executives also use very high filters to send emails directly to the "trash".

However, personalize letters can bypass both of the sentinels cited above. When a secretary gets a personal signed letter there is more of a chance the secretary will pass it onto the boss. Emails are very often "killed" by the sentinel (i.e. the secretary) so it doesn't even get read. Many companies use a high filter in their email system so your email may be detected as spam and will be deleted.

Postcards Can Dominate the Client's Mind

Too many people think if they send just 1 email or 1 letter or 1 postcard it will be enough. I have seen it time and time again a newbie sends out a post card, sit back and wait for the phone to ring. They feel they did something proactive so the prospects should respond.

It doesn't work that way.

To capture someone's attention and to "force" them to remember you it is imperative that you dominate their mind. You need to continually – like perfect clockwork – send them a message periodically. I suggest every 2 weeks or every month.

The easiest way to dominate someone's mind is with an annual postcard campaign. You simply create a very professional, eye catching postcard and have printed in bulk. Create some mailing labels and put them on the cards. You should print out 12 labels for each person on your target mailing list along with a stamp. Then every month simply drop them at the post office.

You will dominate the person's mind. This technique works well for store and restaurant owners, office tenants and professional services.

For example, you may send a post card to a store owner each month that cites how you can help them sell their business; renew their lease, find them a better location, etc. Perhaps each month they may glance at it and throw it away or may keep it on the side in case they need someone like you to help them. But the day they decide to sell they will remember that "real estate professional that sends me a postcard like clockwork every month". They will respect that stick-to-it-tiveness and hope you utilize that type of marketing when you go to sell their business.

Influencers Will Hand Deliver Clients to You

A very important part of your business will come from people you know who will refer business to you. However, they will only refer business to you if you constantly remind them to tell people about you and your services.

The truth of the matter is many good successful people are often busy themselves and can easily forget to refer business prospects to you.

To keep your name and your services on the top of people's minds you need to send them short emails or personal letters letting them know you can help people that are important to THEM.

One of the controversial aspects of having people refer business to you and you referring business to other people is the question of whether or not a referral fee should be involved.

My feeling is that no fee should be involved.

The reason for this is that the person who is referring someone to you truly believes you are top notch and very capable and that is why they are referring their client, family member or friend to you. In addition, most importantly, the prospect that is being referred to you want to know (or believe) that you are being referred to as a great commercial real estate professional because of your abilities not because their colleague, friend or family member is receiving an "under the table" fee. I cite an "under the table" fee because it is very rare that someone will say, "I think you should hire Mr. Smith because he is an excellent commercial real estate professional and by the way Mr. Smith is giving me $500 to recommend Mr. Smith to you".

However, referral fees between a brokerage company and another brokerage company is legal, many companies have pre-printed forms about how to refer business to one another. Please note a real estate agent **cannot** accept a referral fee from another real estate <u>agent</u>. Referrals can only be made from one company to the other company.

So, if you can't pay someone a fee to have them refer business to you, then how do you pay them back?

It is quite simple. You merely make a strong effort to recommend them business back. You may want to send a letter to past and present clients about the integrity and abilities of the person you are trying to help.

Foot Canvassing – Walk Right into the Property

One of the most successful commercial real estate agents in New York became one of the top retail brokers in Manhattan by foot canvassing.

Foot canvassing is basically obtaining a map of an area that you wish to "farm" for retail prospects. Divide the streets up by the days you will be foot canvassing. For example, on Monday from 9 am to 3 pm walk along 2 or 3 key streets and walk into stores. When you enter a store make a mental note if there are a lot of people in that store for that particular hour or if the store seems empty and not doing well.

Then ask for the owner or the General Manager of the store. Introduce yourself (remember the 1 minute elevator speech) and let them know if they ever need help that you are a local expert and can assist them in regard to any real estate requirement they may have and that you can help them sell their business or expand into a larger space.

Be sure you hand them a "leave-behind". A "leave-behind" is a 1-pager that cites the various services you offer and your contact information.

Think about the beauty of this system. Once you start making friends and acquaintances throughout your canvassing you will begin to find out who wants to downsize their space, who wants to expand, who wants to sell and who wants to buy....and they all know you.

This is how you start to put deals together by matching up the right parties. Foot canvassing may be a bit time-consuming but it **IS** certainly worth it.

Giving Lectures

Another effective way to obtain a lot of clients is to give lectures at business associations, chambers of commerce, and other similar organizations.

The key is to become an expert on a particular subject. It is important to truly impart information and genuinely try to teach and help your audience. After the lecture, many attendees will stay afterward to tell you about their particular situation and may ask you how they can hire you.

Websites

A website is a mandatory tool that you will need. In regard to obtaining clients that will hire you as a tenant representative or an investor's representative, it is not very effective. Very few people will simply surf the web and hire someone for a major business decision like leasing a new office or spending hundreds of thousands of dollars.

The website is more of a "validator" meaning that the website validates that you exist and you are a legitimate business.

However, a website can be useful to display exclusive listings. Prospects that are seeking a particular type of property will conduct a search and may lead them to your website listings.

Advertising

The best strategy to find good clients is to have a comprehensive approach. A combination of high-tech tools and "old school" tactics will be very effective. Advertising can be a useful tool to make people more aware of your capabilities, your various services and/or your exclusive listings.

Advertising can be placed in many mediums such as newspapers, magazines, various websites, on line publications, etc.

Chapter 11: Typical Documents

In this chapter you will see some of the templates of some basic forms that are used for Commercial Real Estate.

1. Prospect Form

2. Brokerage Agreement

3. Commission Schedule

4. Proposal to Lease Office Space

5. Retail Lease

6. Commercial Set up

7. Residential Investment Property Set up

8. Restaurant Set Up

9. Floor Plans

INTERNATIONAL PROPERTIES GROUP
Prospect Form

Date received:_____

Source of the lead:_____

COMPANY: _____

Business phone: _____

Exact legal name: _____

PRINCIPAL: _____

Home Phone: _____

Cellular: _____

Address: _____

City: _____

Email: _____

State: _____ Zip: _____

Fax: _____

Type of Business: _____

Credit rating: _____

Years in Business: _____

Sales Volume P/A: _____

Number of Employees: _____

Lease expires: _____

What is the reason for the call?

_____

Who is decision maker?

_____

What is the budget?

_____

Who determines and how is budget determined?

_____

Headquarters or branch office?

_____

How much space?

_____

What type of space layout?

_____

Location?

_____
24/7?
_____BUY_____RENT_____CLASS_____

Have you been using another broker?   _____
        If so, who? _____

Do you have an exclusive?   _____
        If yes, can you send a copy? _____

What problems have you had locating a space?

_____

How long have you been looking?

_____

What buildings have you seen?

_____

What is your knowledge of the market?

_____

What is the best time to look?

_____

Brokerage Agreement

AUTHORIZATION

Dear Sir or Madam:

As of this date_____ we hereby appoint International Properties Group, Inc. (hereinafter referred to as "IPG") as our sole broker granted with the exclusive right to obtain on our behalf or our nominee or designee, a building, space, or interest in a building, whether the procurement thereof is by a new lease, sublease, assignment, license or purchase. All references herein to "us" or "we" means the undersigned and each of our affiliates, designees and subsidiaries.

The term of this Agreement shall be for 1 year and will commence on the above date and <u>may be terminated without cause by either party</u> upon 3 days prior written notice sent to the other party by certified mail, return receipt requested.

You will enlist the best efforts of your firm to secure a location(s) satisfactory to us, and if you deem it necessary you will also solicit the cooperation of other licensed real estate brokers. We will refer to you all inquiries and offerings received by us with respect to the lease or purchase of premises, regardless of the source of such inquires or offerings, and all negotiations shall be conducted solely by you or under your direction, subject to our review and final approval, which may be withheld or withdrawn for any or no reason.

You will acquire the details on all contemplated or presently available locations and carefully select and present to us, at a time convenient to us, those in your opinion are the most suitable for our purposes. If and when we decide on a location, you will negotiate the terms of the purchase or lease on our behalf and in our interest, taking advantage of your knowledge of real estate values and rentals, and the terms of the numerous sales and leases previously negotiated in the market.

Unless otherwise agreed, <u>you will look only to the landlord or seller, as the situation may be, for your commission</u>. Subsequent to the expiration or termination of this Agreement, we shall continue to recognize you as our exclusive broker, in accordance with the provisions hereof, with respect to any prospective locations which have been submitted to us and which appear on a list furnished by you to us within thirty (30) days of the expiration or termination of this Agreement.

The undersigned signatories hereby represent that they are duly authorized to execute this document on behalf of the entity indicated.

This Agreement may be assigned to your successor without our consent.

Any controversy or claim arising out of or relating to this Agreement or the breach thereof, shall be settled by arbitration in New York City in accordance with the rules and regulations of the American Arbitration Association. However, each party shall be entitled to discovery pursuant to Article 31 of the Civil Practice Laws and Rules.

This Agreement shall be binding upon the parties hereto and their respective successors and assigns.

If the foregoing accurately sets forth our Agreement, please sign and return the enclosed copies of this letter.

Very truly yours,

BUYER/TENANT

By:_____

Name:_____

Title: _____

READ, AGREED TO AND ACCEPTED:
International Properties Group, Inc.

_____

By: George F. Donohue
PRESIDENT

Commission Schedule

VALUE, TRUST AND EXPERTISE

Exhibit A

OFFICE LEASES

On the rental for all or any fraction of:

The first, second years..	5%
The third year	4%
The fourth, fifth, sixth and seventh year	3%
The eighth, ninth and tenth year	2.5%
The eleventh year and beyond	2%

RETAIL LEASES

On the rental for all or any fraction of:

The first	6%
The second year	5%
The third, fourth, fifth years	4%
The sixth through tenth years	3%
The eleventh through twentieth years	2%
The twenty-first year and beyond	1%

For selling furniture, fixtures and/or good will (retail and office)......10%

TERMS AND CONDITIONS

1. All commissions payable hereunder shall be computed upon the base or fixed annual rent, (hereinafter referred to as the "Base Rent") payable by a Tenant under a Lease and upon real estate taxes and operating expenses paid by a net lessee under a net lease and in no event shall the following be subject to Agent's commission: (i) electric charges, (ii) any escalation payments made by tenant pursuant to increases in real estate taxes, fuel, operating expenses, labor. On leases where there is an allowance in the form of rental concession (as distinguished from an allowance for repairs and decoration, etc.) the commission shall be calculated on the net rental for

the term. The calculation of a full commission payable, and the rental not payable by reason of the concession shall be ratably spread over the entire term of the Lease.

2.   Notwithstanding the commission rates herein in the event that term of any Lease shall be two years or less the commission will be 10% of the aggregate rental.

3.   If the Lease provides for an option to cancel by the Proposed Tenant, the Agent shall be paid a commission calculated and paid in accordance with the terms and rates as set forth herein for the term of the Lease not subject to such option and the remainder of the commission shall be paid to the Agent in the event the option to cancel is not exercised or waived. Notwithstanding the foregoing, in the event that the option to cancel by Tenant contains a cancellation penalty which includes the unamortized portion of Agent's commission, Agent shall be paid a commission based on the entire term of the Lease, disregarding any term which may be cancelable pursuant to said option or right. A Lease shall be deemed to be canceled only if the Tenant vacates the premises. If the cancellation is by mutual agreement not contained in the Lease as originally executed, or if the Lease gives the

Proposed Tenant the right or option to cancel by reason of the Landlord's act or omission to act, Broker shall be paid a full commission.

4.   If there is a clause in the Lease which gives a Tenant an option to purchase the property or of a first refusal, and if the Tenant or its designee, successor or assignee, exercises such option, then Principal shall, at the time of passing title, pay a sales commission to Agent, in accordance with the schedule of sales commissions set forth in article 7.

5.   Should there be a clause in a Lease whereby Tenant is obligated to pay the real property taxes such taxes shall be considered as rent on which Agent's commission is payable. In making the computation, the taxes for current year, if fixed, shall be used; if not fixed, the taxes for the previous year shall be used. However, where new construction is involved, that

152

portion of the commission based on real estate taxes shall be computed and paid on the basis of the real estate tax bill rendered for the first full year for which the Premises shall have been assessed as a completed functioning Premises.

6.   With respect to percentage Leases: commissions shall be due and payable in the specified manner on the minimum rental, or if there be none, then, in any event, computed on not less than 65% of the asking price. Agent shall be notified promptly with regard to rent paid during the term in addition to the minimum rent. The commission on such additional rent shall be computed as if the amount thereof had been known at the time the Lease was executed. Such computation and payment shall be done on an annual basis.

7.   With respect to selling or exchanging real estate, the commission rate on the transaction will be 6% of the selling price.

Proposal to Lease Office Space

June 24th, 2019

Mr. Alexander Smith
Associate Real Estate Broker
ABC Company
205 East 42nd street
New York, NY 10017

Re: Proposal to lease full Fourth floor at 567 Third Avenue.

Dear Mr. Frost,

Our exclusive client, **Gold Shield Foundation** is currently located at 870 United Nations Plaza and has authorized us to submit the following proposal:

BUILDING:	567 Third Avenue New York, New York 10016
TENANT:	Shield Foundation
TAX ID #:	ID # 13-1234567
SPACE:	Full Fourth floor
AREA:	1,800 rentable square feet

USE:	General, administrative and executive offices
TERM:	Ten years
BASE RENT:	$5,400 per month with an escalation of 3% a year.
POSSESSION AND LEASE COMMENCEMENT:	August 1, 2019
RENT COMMENCES:	December 1, 2019
LANDLORD'S WORK:	None
SECURITY DEPOSIT:	$10,800
	Security Deposit will burn down if Tenant has a good payment history. One month Security Deposit will be returned after 12 months of good payment history.
ELECTRIC & HVAC:	Electric directly metered.
TAX ESCALATIONS:	RE taxes are 20% of increases over the base year (2017/2018).

SUBLEASING AND ASSIGNMENT:	Tenant shall have the right to assign or sublease any portion, or the entire premises upon written consent of Landlord, not to be unreasonably withheld. Tenant may assign or sublease the premises to any and all affiliates without the Landlord's consent.
CLEANING:	Tenant will be responsible for cleaning. Tenant can retain outside cleaners or contract with the building's cleaners directly.
TENANT LAWYER:	Edwin Jones
	c/o The Gold Shield Foundation
	870 Main Street
	New York, NY 10017
BROKERAGE:	Landlord shall pay International Properties Group one (1) full commission at lease signing. (See attached standard Commission Schedule).

This proposal is submitted to you in strict confidence for negotiation purposes only. It is subject to final review and approval of tenant and it's Board of Directors.

We look forward to your favorable response and assure you of our full cooperation.

Very truly yours,

_____

George F. Donohue, President
International Properties Group

Agreed to by Landlord or Authorized Representative:

Printed name:

_____

Signature:

_____

Title:

_____

Address:

_____

_____

_____

Phone:

_____

Fax:

_____

Enclosure: Commission Schedule
               Financial Statements

Retail Lease

VALUE, TRUST AND EXPERTISE

TERM SHEET

1. **Building Address:** 1234 Greenwich Street, New York, NY 10006

2. **Landlord:** 1234 Greenwich Street Owner

3. **Tenant:** ABC Corporation

4. **Premises:**

a. **Floor(s):** 2nd Floor and partial basement

b. **RSF per floor:** 2nd Floor: 2,300 SF

Basement: Storage space to be assigned by landlord

5. **Term** 10 years with one (1) Five-year option.

6. Lease Commencement Date: January 1, 2019.

7. Rent Starts: 2 months following NYC Building Department approval.

8. Base Rent: The rent will be $9,500 per month for the first 10 years. It will increase to $10,000 per month when the XYZ Center officially opens.

9. Use/Purpose: Any retail and/or food use and/or office use

10. Condition of Premises:

a. All services stubbed to Tenants specifications. Tenant will provide drawings of proposed floor plan with utility locations 10 calendar days after lease signing.

b. Landlord to install all finished ceiling, framing and sheetrock necessary to deliver the premises as a "plain vanilla box" broom-cleaned.

c. Landlord will deliver finished bathroom facilities up to code.

d. Landlord will provide a dedicated 220 electrical service and necessary electrical outlets and switches with switch plates and covers to standard.

11. Electricity: Direct meter

12. Tenant Construction & Alterations:

a. Tenant to have the right to do all of its finishing work and installation of trade fixtures both initially and in the future.

b. Tenant shall provide Landlord with Tenant's plans for Landlord's review and reasonable approval.

c. During Tenant's initial alterations, Landlord shall not charge for use of freight elevators, nor for any stub-in charges for connecting supplemental air conditioning, sprinklers, etc.

13. Sublet & Assignment:

a. Tenant shall have the right at any time to sublease or assign any portion or all of Tenant's Premises to any unrelated entities with Landlord's consent, not to be unreasonably withheld, conditioned or delayed.

14. Building Security:

a. Landlord, at Landlord's sole cost and expense, shall provide building security, equipment, procedures and systems.

b. The building has 24-hour access.

15. Signage:

a. Tenant to abide by building signage requirements

b. Any scaffolding set-up in front of the property shall automatically begin a free rent period until scaffolding is removed.

18. Security Deposit: 3 months

19. Sale/Hotel: In the event the tenant exercises their 5 year option and the Landlord wishes to sell the building or convert its use during that extended period, the landlord will give the Tenant a 6 months' notice.

If the Landlord gives notice to sell or convert in the following years, the Landlord will pay the Tenant the corresponding amounts to vacate their space.

Year 11	$100,000
Year 12	80,000
Year 13	60,000
Year 14	40,000
Year 15	20,000

20. Brokerage: International Properties Group will be paid on lease signing one (1) full

161

commission based upon a separate agreement.

Agreed to by:

Tenant

Signature: _____

Title: _____

Date: _____

Agreed to by:

Landlord or Landlord Representative

Signature: _____

Title: _____

Date: _____

162

Commercial Set Up

EXCLUSIVELY LISTED BY
INTERNATIONAL PROPERTIES GROUP

**Outstanding
Office/Medical Facility**

For Sale

2565 Route 9W
Cornwall, NY 12518

Asking Price: $1,100,000

Highlights

- 7252 Square feet
- Free-standing building
- Private parking
- Excellent condition
- High visibility –
  13,500 daily traffic court
- Easy access to area hospitals
- Equipped for radiology/oncology
- 11 Office/Exam rooms
- 2 Conference rooms
- 3 Radiology procedure rooms
- 6 bathrooms
- 2nd story storage area
- Waiting and reception areas

- 10 miles to West Point
- 10 miles to Stewart Int. Airport
- 50 miles to G.W. Bridge
- Equipment list available
- Located on 1.08 acres
- 220 volts/3 phase electricity
- Previous Doctor grossed 3m/year
- Building can easily be divided
- New medical equipment valued over $1.4M
- Equipment can be purchased
- State of the art medical construction
- Also, great for an investor
- Rental income can generate $127,500 per year

Listed By:

Teresa Vela-Hayes
Managing Director –
Sales & Leasing
(845) 742-6816
tvelahayesipg@gmail.com

IPG REAL ESTATE

VALUE, TRUST AND EXPERIENCE

Call with questions & to schedule a tour.

International Properties Group does not guarantee the information contained herein, and same is subject to change, errors or omissions by the principals. You are advised to independently verify this information through personal inspection or with the appropriate professionals.

163

Residential Investment Setup

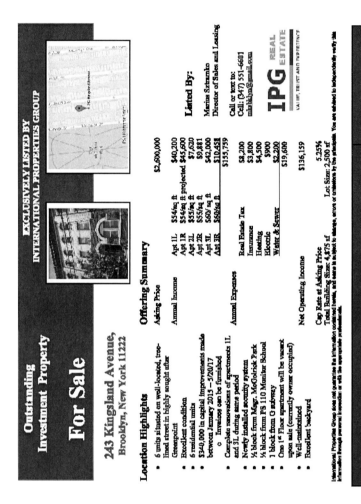

Outstanding Investment Property

EXCLUSIVELY LISTED BY
INTERNATIONAL PROPERTIES GROUP

For Sale

243 Kingsland Avenue,
Brooklyn, New York 11222

Listed By:

Marius Sztramko
Director of Sales and Leasing

Call or text to:
Cell: (347) 551-6601
mtsztklpg@gmail.com

IPG REAL ESTATE

VALUE, TRUST AND EXPERIENCE

www.realestateipg.com

Location Highlights

- 6 units situated on well-looked, tree-lined street in highly sought after Greenpoint
- Excellent condition
- 6 residential units
- $340,000 in capital improvements made between January 2015 – 5/20/17
  - Invoices can be furnished
- Complete renovations of apartments 1L and 3L during same period
- Newly installed security system
- ½ block from Msgr. McGolrick Park
- ½ block from PS 110 Monitor School
- 1 block from G subway
- One 1st Floor apartment will be vacant upon sale (currently owner occupied)
- Well-maintained
- Excellent backyard

Offering Summary

Asking Price			$2,600,000
Annual Income			
	Apt 1L	$54/sq ft	$40,200
	Apt 1R	$54/sq ft projected	$45,600
	Apt 2L	$55/sq ft	$7,620
	Apt 2R	$55/sq ft	$9,881
	Apt 3L	$60/ sq ft	$42,000
	Apt 3R	$60/sq ft	$10,458
			$155,759
Annual Expenses			
	Real Estate Tax		$8,200
	Insurance		$3,800
	Heating		$4,500
	Electric		$900
	Water & Sewer		$2,200
			$19,600
Net Operating Income			$136,159

Cap Rate at Asking Price: 5.25%
Total Building Size: 4,875 sf   Lot Size: 2,500 sf

International Properties Group does not guarantee the information contained herein, and same is subject to change, errors or omissions by the standards. You are advised to independently verify this information through persons licensed or sell the appropriate professionals.

Listing Office: IPG REAL ESTATE   122 West 27th Street 11 floor, New York, New York 10001

164

High-End Restaurant for Sale

132 E 61st St
New York, NY 10065

EXCLUSIVELY LISTED BY INTERNATIONAL PROPERTIES GROUP

AVAILABLE
FOR SALE
Key Money: $350,000

Property Details

- Owned and operated by a reputable French Chef
- Newly built
- Elegant, clean interior
- Gross Income: $11.3M
- $400,000 in capital improvements recently spent on interior
- 2,000 square feet on first floor
- Very large basement
- Rent: $28,000/month
- 8 years remaining on lease

Neighbors Include

AUGUST

Sushi by Melissa

THE BAR ROOM

GINZA Sushi Restaurant

Wajima

Listed By:

Keith Radhuber
Managing Director

Call or text to:
Cell: (848) 667-6622
kradhuber@realestateipg.com

IPG REAL ESTATE

VALUE, TRUST AND EXPERIENCE

www.realestateipg.com

Listing Office: IPG REAL ESTATE 122 West 27th Street 11 floor, New York, New York 10001

EXHIBIT A

FLOOR PLAN

EAST 61ST STREET

166

Floor Plans

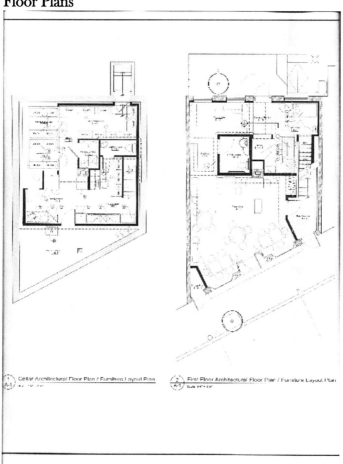

1 / A-1 Cellar Architectural Floor Plan / Furniture Layout Plan

2 / A-1 First Floor Architectural Floor Plan / Furniture Layout Plan

Chapter 12: Conclusion

Conclusion

I hope my book has given you some insight into all the opportunities, challenges and issues related to working in the field of commercial real estate.

I think after you have read this book you can see commercial real estate is quite different than residential real estate. I believe there are many more roads to travel in the life of a commercial real estate professional. Those roads can be quite interesting, exciting and lucrative.

I tried to provide you with knowledge about the tools and skills you will need to acquire or to hone to become successful at the craft of commercial real estate and to be happy in your pursuit.

One thing is certain; you never want to be a "would of, could of, should of" person. If this book has enlightencd you to a profession you believe you can be good at, then by all means go for it.

If this book has shed light on opportunities and issues you have never before conceived and it has made you rethink your life's goals but you still are uncertain about a career in commercial real estate then I urge you to look into the subjects cited in this book that may be making you apprehensive. Learn as much as you can about the particular areas. This will give you the confidence to make a decision that is best for you.

Whether you choose to stay in residential real estate or try commercial real estate the most important recommendation about your future can be found in the words of the famous American philosopher Joseph Campbell; "Follow your bliss"!

(The following is the full excerpt from Joseph Campbell: *"If you follow your bliss, you put yourself on a kind of track that has been there all the while, waiting for you, and the life that you ought to be living is the one you are living. Wherever you are — if you are following your bliss, you are enjoying that refreshment, that life within you, all the time."*)

Chapter 13: Final Self-Assessment and Action Plan

The following is a self-assessment to help you decide if a career in commercial real estate is right for you. Now that you have read the book the questions in this self-assessment are posed:

To help you reflect upon the decision.

To help you decide if this is realistic for you.

To help you decide if it is doable in regard to your present situation.

American Deal Makers Series

Crossing Over

Self Assessment

Name: _____

Today's Date: _____

1. After reading the first part of this book my general thoughts on Crossing Over are:
   a. _____
   b. _____

2. The following best describes my present situation:

    a. _____ I absolutely love doing residential real estate but am interested in commercial

    b. _____ Residential Real Estate brokerage is okay; I need to do something else

    c. _____ I absolutely do not like Residential Real Estate brokerage

    d. _____ I believe Commercial Real Estate is the right career for me

    e. _____ Other (Describe:

_____

3. The following describes my intention thus far:

    a. _____ I will definitely Cross Over and pursue Commercial Real Estate

    b. _____ I am more confident about Crossing Over into Commercial Real Estate

    c. _____ I am still not sure

4. In regard to learning new Tools for the Trade check off the box that applies:

    a. Blue print reading

        i. _____ I already know this

        ii. _____ I can learn this

        iii. _____ I intend to learn this but am not sure where to get the training

    iv. _____ This is too difficult for me to learn

b. Understanding Demographics
    i. _____ I already know this
    ii. _____ I can learn this
    iii. _____ I intend to learn this but am not sure where to get the training
    iv. _____ This is too difficult for me to learn

c. Excel Spreadsheets
    i. _____ I already know this
    ii. _____ I can learn this
    iii. _____ I intend to learn this but am not sure where to get the training
    iv. _____ This is too difficult for me to learn

d. Basics of Contract Law
    i. _____ I already know this
    ii. _____ I can learn this
    iii. _____ I intend to learn this but am not sure where to get the training
    iv. _____ This is too difficult for me to learn

e. Basics of Construction and Architecture
    i. _____ I already know this

      ii. _____ I can learn this

      iii. _____ I intend to learn this but am not sure where to get the training

      iv. _____ This is too difficult for me to learn

f. Evaluating the Value of a Commercial Property

      i. _____ I already know this

      ii. _____ I can learn this

      iii. _____ I intend to learn this but am not sure where to get the training

      iv. _____ This is too difficult for me to learn

g. Conducting Commercial Research

      i. _____ I already know this

      ii. _____ I can learn this

      iii. _____ I intend to learn this but am not sure where to get the training

      iv. _____ This is too difficult for me to learn

h. Prospecting for Commercial Clients

      i. _____ I already know this

      ii. _____ I can learn this

      iii. _____ I intend to learn this but am not sure where to get the training

iv. _____ This is too difficult for me to learn

i. Marketing Tactics related to Commercial Clients
    i. _____ I already know this
    ii. _____ I can learn this
    iii. _____ I intend to learn this but am not sure where to get the training
    iv. _____ This is too difficult for me to learn

j. Qualifying Businesses and Investors
    i. _____ I already know this
    ii. _____ I can learn this
    iii. _____ I intend to learn this but am not sure where to get the training
    iv. _____ This is too difficult for me to learn

k. Negotiating
    i. _____ I already know this
    ii. _____ I can learn this
    iii. _____ I intend to learn this but am not sure where to get the training
    iv. _____ This is too difficult for me to learn

l. Time Management

i. _____ I already know this
ii. _____ I can learn this
iii. _____ I intend to learn this but am not sure where to get the training
iv. _____ This is too difficult for me to learn

m. Networking
i. _____ I already know this
ii. _____ I can learn this
iii. _____ I intend to learn this but am not sure where to get the training
iv. _____ This is too difficult for me to learn

n. Proposal Writing
i. _____ I already know this
ii. _____ I can learn this
iii. _____ I intend to learn this but am not sure where to get the training
iv. _____ This is too difficult for me to learn

5. In regard to perhaps working on a commercial real estate team. How does this best describe your feelings:
a. _____ I prefer to always work alone
b. _____ I would be open to working on a team

c. _____ I definitely would be interested in working on a team.

6. I am most interested in representing these types of commercial clients: (Check off all that apply):
    a. _____ Office Tenants
    b. _____ Retail Tenants
    c. _____ Warehouse Tenants
    d. _____ Pop-Up Stores
    e. _____ Office Building Owners
    f. _____ Strip Mall Owners
    g. _____ Investors
    h. _____ Land Owners Seeking a Buyer
    i. _____ Doctors, Lawyers and Professional Services
    j. _____ Manufacturers
    k. _____ Government Agencies
    l. _____ Others
    (_____)

7. Which type of firm would you prefer? Please state why.
    a. _____ A large firm.
    _____
    b. _____ A small firm.
    _____

8. I am interested in Crossing Over for the following reasons: Check all that apply.
    a. _____ I need to make more money for me and/or my family

176

b. _____ I need more of a challenge
c. _____ I am presently and/or not satisfied with my present career
d. _____ I was always fascinated with commercial real estate and want to try it

Conclusion and Directions:

Now that you have checked off all the answers, go back and carefully look over the results. It should give you some indication on what direction you should take in pursuing a career in Commercial Real Estate.

I urge you to take these answers and discuss them with your spouse, partner, family, friends, perhaps even with your therapist (if you have one.).

People who care about you and truly know your personality and abilities will also give you some good advice.

Continue reading and perhaps at the end of the book your intentions and planning may change.

Glossary

A

abstract of title A summary of all of the recorded instruments and proceedings that affect the title to property, arranged in the order in which they were recorded

accretion The addition of land through processes of nature, as by water or wind

accrued interest Accrue; to grow; to be added to. Accrued interest is interest that has been earned but not due and payable.

acknowledgment A formal declaration before a duly authorized officer by a person who has executed an instrument that such execution is the person's act and deed

acquisition An act or process by which a person procures property

acre A measure of land equaling 43,560 square feet

action for specific performance A court action to compel a defaulting principal to comply with the provisions of a contract

Glossary

adjacent Lying near to but not necessarily in actual contact with

adjoining Contiguous; attaching, in actual contact with

administrator A person appointed by the court to administer the estate of a deceased person who left no will; i.e., who died intestate

ad valorem According to valuation

adverse possession A means of acquiring title where an occupant has been in actual, open, notorious, exclusive, and continuous occupancy of property under a claim of right for the required statutory period

affidavit A statement or declaration reduced to writing and sworn to or affirmed before some officer who is authorized to administer an oath or affirmation

affirm To confirm, to ratify, to verify

agency That relationship between principal and agent that arises out of a contract either expressed or implied, written or oral, wherein an agent is employed by a person to do certain acts on the person's behalf in dealing with a third party

Glossary

agent One who undertakes to transact some business or to manage some affair for another by authority of the latter

agreement of sale A written agreement between seller and purchaser in which the purchaser agrees to buy certain real estate and the seller agrees to sell upon terms and conditions set forth therein

air rights Rights in real property to use the space above the surface of the land

alienation A transferring of property to another; the transfer of property and possession of lands, or other things, from one person to another

alienation clause Allows a lender to require the balance of a loan to be paid in full if the collateral is sold (also known as a "due on sale" clause)

amortization A gradual paying off of a debt by periodic installments

apportionment Adjustment of the income, expenses, or carrying charges of real estate usually computed to the date of closing of title so that the seller pays all expenses to that date. The buyer assumes all expenses commencing the date the deed is conveyed to the buyer.

Glossary

appraisal An estimate of a property's value by an appraiser who is usually presumed to be expert in his or her work

appraisal by cost approach Adding together all parts of a property separately appraised to form a whole; e.g., the value of the land considered as vacant added to the cost of reproduction of the building, less depreciation

appraisal by income capitalization approach An estimate of value by capitalization of productivity and income

appraisal by sale comparison approach Comparability with the sales prices of other similar properties

appurtenance Something that is outside the property itself but belongs to the land and adds to its greater enjoyment, such as a right-of-way or a barn or a dwelling

assessed valuation A valuation placed upon property by a public officer or a board, as a basis for taxation

assessment A charge against real estate made by a unit of government to cover a proportionate cost of an improvement, such as a street or sewer

assessor An official who has the responsibility of determining assessed values

Glossary

assignee The person to whom an agreement or contract is assigned

assignment The method or manner by which a right or contract is transferred from one person to another

assignor A party who assigns or transfers an agreement or contract to another

assumption of mortgage The taking of title to property by a grantee, wherein the grantee assumes liability for payment of an existing note or bond secured by a mortgage against a property and becomes personally liable for the payment of such mortgage debt

avulsion A sudden and perceptible loss or addition to land by the action of water, or a sudden change in the bed or course of a stream

B

balloon mortgage payment A large payment during the term of a mortgage, often at the end

beneficiary The person who receives or is to receive the benefits resulting from certain acts

bequeath To give or hand down by will; to leave by will

bequest That which is given by the terms of a will

bill of sale A written instrument given to pass title of personal property from vendor to vendee

binder An agreement to cover the down payment for the purchase of real estate as evidence of good faith on the part of the purchaser

blanket mortgage A mortgage covering more than one property. A blanket mortgage is often used for subdivision financing.

blockbusting The practice of inducing homeowners in a particular neighborhood to sell their homes quickly, often at below market prices, by creating the fear that the entry of a minority group or groups into the neighborhood will cause a precipitous decline in property values

bona fide In good faith, without fraud

bond The evidence of a personal debt that is secured by a mortgage or other lien on real estate

building code Regulations established by state or local governments stating fully the structural requirements for building

building line A line fixed at a certain distance from the front and/or sides of a lot, beyond which no building can project

building loan agreement An agreement whereby the lender advances money to an owner primarily in the erection of buildings. Such funds are commonly advanced in installments as the structure is completed.

building permit Written governmental permission for the construction, renovation, or substantial repair of a building

C

cancellation clause A provision in a lease or other contract that confers upon one or more of all of the parties to the lease the right to terminate the party's or parties' obligations thereunder upon the occurrence of the condition or contingency set forth in the said clause

capital appreciation The appreciation accruing to the benefit of the capital improvement to real estate

capital asset Any asset of a permanent nature used for the production of income

Glossary

capital gain Income that results from the sale of an asset not in the usual course of business. (Capital gains may be taxed at a lower rate than ordinary income.)

capital improvement Any structure erected as a permanent improvement to real estate, usually extending the useful life and value of a property. (The replacement of a roof would be considered a capital improvement.)

capital loss A loss from the sale of an asset not in the usual course of business

caveat emptor Let the buyer beware. The buyer must examine the goods or property and buy at the buyer's own risk.

cease and desist list Upon the establishment of a cease and desist zone by the Secretary, a list of homeowners who have filed owner's statements expressing their wish not to be solicited by real estate brokers or salespersons. Soliciting of listed homeowners by licensees is prohibited. Violators of such prohibition are subject to licensure suspension or revocation.

Glossary

cease and desist zone A rule adopted by the Secretary of State that prohibits the direct solicitation of homeowners whose names and addresses appear on a cease and desist list maintained by the Secretary. Such rule may be adopted upon the Secretary's determination that some homeowners within a defined geographic area have been subject to intense and repeated solicitation by real estate brokers and salespersons.

certificate of occupancy (CO) A document issued by a governmental authority that a building is ready and fit for occupancy

chain of title A history of conveyances and encumbrances affecting a title from the time the original patent was granted, or as far back as records are available

chattel Personal property, such as household goods

client The one by whom a broker is employed

closing date The date upon which the property is conveyed by the seller to the buyer

cloud on the title An outstanding claim or encumbrance that, if valid, would affect or impair the owner's title

collateral Additional security pledged for the payment of an obligation

Glossary

color of title That which appears to be good title, but that is not title in fact

commingling To mingle or mix, for example, a client's funds in the broker's personal or general account

commission A sum due a real estate broker for services in that capacity

commitment A pledge or a promise; affirmation agreement

completion bond A bond used to guarantee that a proposed subdivision development will be completed

condemnation Taking private property for public use, with fair compensation to the owner; exercising the right of eminent domain

conditional sales contract A contract for the sale of property stating that delivery is to be made to the buyer, title to remain vested in the seller until the conditions of the contract have been fulfilled

consideration Anything given to induce another to enter into a con- tract, such as money or personal services

Glossary

constructive notice Information or knowledge of a fact imputed by law to a person because the person could have discovered the fact by proper diligence and inquiry(e.g., via public records)

contingency A provision in a contract that requires the occurrence of a specific event before the contract can be completed

contract An agreement between competent parties to do or not to do certain things that is legally enforceable, whereby each party acquires a right

conversion Change from one character or use to another

conveyance The transfer of the title of land from one to another; the means or medium by which title of real estate is transferred

covenants Agreements written into deeds and other instruments promising performance or nonperformance of certain acts, or stipulating certain uses or non-uses of the property

cul-de-sac A blind alley; a street with only one outlet

current value The value usually sought to be estimated in an appraisal

Glossary

D

damages The indemnity recoverable by a person who has sustained an injury, either to his or her person, property, or relative rights, through the act or default of another

debit The amount charged as due or owed

duress Unlawful constraint exercised upon a person whereby the person is forced to do some act against the person's will

E

earnest money Down payment made by a purchaser of real estate as evidence of good faith

easement A right that may be exercised by the public or individuals on, over, or through the lands of others

economic life The period over which a property will yield the investor a return on the investment

Glossary

economic obsolescence Lessened desirability or useful life arising from economic forces, such as changes in optimum land use, legislative enactments that restrict or impair property rights, and changes in supply-demand ratios

ejectment A form of action to regain possession of real property, with damages for the unlawful retention; used when there is no relationship of landlord and tenant

eminent domain A right of the government to acquire property for necessary public use by condemnation; the owner must be fairly compensated

encroachment A building, part of a building, or obstruction that intrudes upon or invades a highway or sidewalk or trespasses upon the property of another

encumbrance Any right to or interest in the land interfering with its use or transfer, or subjecting it to an obligation (Also *incumbrance)*

endorsement An act of signing one's name on the back of a check or note, with or without further qualifications

equity The interest or value that the owner has in real estate over and above the liens against it

equity loan Junior loan based on a percentage of the equity

Glossary

equity of redemption A right of the owner to reclaim property before it is sold through foreclosure proceedings, by the payment of the debt, interest, and costs

erosion The wearing away of land through processes of nature, as by water and winds

escheat The reversion to the State of property in the event the owner thereof abandons it or dies, without leaving a will and has no distributees to whom the property may pass by lawful descent

escrow A written agreement between two or more parties providing that certain instruments or property be placed with a third party to be delivered to a designated person upon the fulfillment or performance of some act or condition

estate The degree, quantity, nature, and extent of interest that a person has in real property

estate at will The occupation of lands and tenements by a tenant for an indefinite period, terminable by one or both parties at will

estate in reversion The residue of an estate left for the grantor, to commence in possession after the termination of some particular estate granted by the grantor

Glossary

estoppel certificate An instrument executed by the mortgagor setting forth the present status and the balance due on the mortgage as of the date of the execution of the certificate

eviction A legal proceeding by a landlord to recover possession of real property from a tenant

eviction, actual Where one is, either by force or by process of law, actually put out of possession

eviction, constructive Any disturbance of the tenant's possession of the leased premises by the landlord whereby the premises are rendered unfit or unsuitable for the purpose for which they were leased

exclusive agency An agreement of employment of a broker to the exclusion of all other brokers; if sale is made by any other broker during term of employment, broker holding exclusive agency is entitled to commissions in addition to the commissions payable to the broker who *effected* the transaction

exclusive right to sell An agreement of employment by a broker under which the exclusive right to sell for a specified period is granted to the broker; if a sale during the term of the agreement is made by the owner or by any other broker, the broker holding such exclusive right to sell is nevertheless entitled to compensation

Glossary

executor A male person or a corporate entity or any other type of organization named or designed in a will to carry out its provisions as to the disposition of the estate of a deceased person

executrix A woman appointed to perform the same duties as an executor

extension agreement An agreement that extends the life of a mortgage to a later date

F

fee; fee simple; fee absolute Absolute ownership of real property; a person has this type of estate where the person is entitled to the entire property with unconditional power of disposition during the person's life and descending to the person's heirs or distributees

fiduciary A person who, on behalf of or for the benefit of another, transacts business or handles money or property not the person's own; such relationship implies great confidence and trust

fixtures Personal property so attached to the land or improvements as to become part of the real property

foreclosure A procedure whereby property pledged as security for a debt is sold to pay the debt in the event of default in payments or terms

freehold An interest in real estate, not less than an estate for life. (Use of this term discontinued September 1, 1967.)

G

grace period Additional time allowed to perform an act or make a payment before a default occurs

graduated leases A lease that provides for a graduated change at stated intervals in the amount of the rent to be paid; used largely in long-term leases

grant A technical term used in deeds of conveyance of lands to indicate a transfer

grantee The party to whom the title to real property is conveyed

grantor The person who conveys real estate by deed; the seller

Glossary

gross income Total income from property before any expenses are deducted

gross lease A lease of property whereby the lessor is to meet all property charges regularly incurred through ownership

ground rent Earnings of improved property credited to earnings of the ground itself after allowance made for earnings of improvements

group boycott An agreement between members of a trade to exclude other members from fair participation in the trade

H

habendum clause The "to have and to hold" clause that defines or limits the quantity of the estate granted in the premises of the deed

holdover tenant A tenant who remains in possession of leased property after the expiration of the lease term

Glossary

I

incompetent A person who is unable to manage his or her own affairs by reason of insanity, imbecility, or feeblemindedness

in rem A proceeding against the realty directly; as distinguished from a proceeding against a person (Used in taking land for nonpayment of taxes, etc.)

installments Parts of the same debt, payable at successive periods as·agreed; payments made to reduce a mortgage

instrument A written legal document; created to *effect* the rights of the parties

interest rate The percentage of a sum of money charged for its use

intestate A person who dies having made no will, or leaves one that is defective in form, in which case the person's estate descends to the person's distributees in the manner prescribed by law

involuntary lien A lien imposed against property without consent of the owner, such as taxes, special assessments

Glossary

irrevocable Incapable of being recalled or revoked; unchangeable; unalterable

J

joint tenancy Ownership of realty by two or more persons, each of whom has an undivided interest with the "right of survivorship"

judgment A formal decision issued by a court concerning the respective rights and claims of the parties to an act or suit

junior mortgage A mortgage second in lien to a previous mortgage

L

laches Delay or negligence in asserting one's legal rights; landlord One who rents property to another

Glossary

lease A contract whereby, for a consideration, usually termed rent, one who is entitled to the possession of real property transfers such rights to another for life, for a term of years, or at will

leasehold The interest or estate that a lessee of real estate has therein by virtue of the lessee's lease

lessee A person to whom property is rented under a lease lessor One who rents property to another under a lease

lien A legal right or claim upon a specific property that attaches to the property until a debt is satisfied

life estate The conveyance of title to property for the duration of the life of the grantee

life tenant The holder of a life estate

lis pendens A legal document, filed in the office of the county clerk, giving notice that an auction or proceeding is pending in the courts affecting the title to the property. (Not applicable in commission disputes.)

listing An employment contract between principal and agent, authorizing the agent to perform services for the principal involving the latter's property

Glossary

littoral rights The right of a property owner whose land borders on a body of water, such as a lake, ocean, or sea, to reasonable use and enjoyment of the shore and water the property borders on

M

Mandatory Requiring strict conformity or obedience

marketable title A title that a court of equity considers to be so free from defect that it will enforce its acceptance by a purchaser

market allocation An agreement between members of a trade to refrain from competition in specific market areas

market price The actual selling price of a property

market value The most probable price that a property should bring if exposed for sale in the open market for a reasonable period of time, with both the buyer and seller aware of current market conditions, neither being under duress

Glossary

mechanic's lien A lien given by law upon a building or other improvement upon land, and upon the land itself, to secure the price of labor done upon, and materials furnished for, the improvement

meeting of the minds Whenever all parties to a contract agree to the substance and terms thereof

metes and bounds A term used in describing the boundary lines of land, seeing forth all the boundary lines together with their terminal points and angles

minor A person under an age specified by law; usually under 18 years of age

monument A fixed object and point established by surveyors to establish land locations

mortgage An instrument in writing, duly executed and delivered, that creates a lien upon real estate as security for the payment of a specified debt, which is usually in the form of a bond

mortgage commitment A formal indication by a lending institution that it will grant a mortgage loan on property in a certain specified amount and on certain specified terms

mortgagee The party who lends money and takes a mortgage to secure the payment thereof

mortgage reduction certificate An instrument executed by the mortgagee, setting forth the present status and the balance due on the mortgage as of the date of the execution of the instrument

mortgagor A person who borrows money and gives a mortgage on the person's property as security for the payment of the debt

multiple listing An arrangement among Real Estate Board of Exchange members, whereby each broker presents the broker's listings to the attention of the other members so that if a sale results, the commission is divided between the broker bringing the listing and the broker making the sale

N

net listing A price below which an owner will not sell the property, and at which price a broker will not receive a commission; the broker receives the excess over and above the net listing as the broker's commission

Glossary

non-solicitation order A rule adopted by the Secretary of State that prohibits any or all types of solicitation directed toward homeowners within a defined geographic area. Such rule may be adopted after a public hearing and upon the Secretary's determination that homeowners within the subject area have been subject to intense and repeated solicitations by real estate brokers or salespersons and that such solicitations have caused owners to reasonably believe that property values may decrease because persons of different race, ethnic, religious, or social backgrounds are moving or about to move into such area.

notary public A public officer who is authorized to take acknowledgments to certain classes of documents, such as deeds, contracts, and mortgages, and before whom affidavits may be sworn

O

Oblige The person in whose favor an obligation is entered into obligor The person who binds himself or herself to another; one who has engaged to perform some obligation; one who makes a bond

obsolescence Loss in value due to reduced desirability and usefulness of a structure because its design and construction become obsolete; loss because of becoming old fashioned, and not in keeping with modern means, with consequent loss of income

open listing A listing given to any number of brokers without liability to compensate any except the one who first secures a buyer ready, willing, and able to meet the terms of the listing, or secures the acceptance by the seller of a satisfactory offer; the sale of the property automatically terminates the listing

option A right given for a consideration to purchase or lease a property upon specified terms within a specified time; if the right is not exercised the option holder is not subject to liability for damages; if exercised, the grantor of option must perform

P

partition The division that is made of real property between those who own it in undivided shares

Glossary

party wall A wall built along the line separating two properties, partly on each, which either owner, the owner's heirs, and assigns have the right to use; such right constituting an easement over so much of the adjoining owner's land as is covered by the wall

percentage lease A lease of property in which the rental is based upon the percentage of the volume of sales made upon the leased premises; usually provides for minimum rental

performance bond A bond used to guarantee the specific completion of an endeavor in accordance with a contract

personal property Any property that is not real property

plat book A public record containing maps of land showing the division of such land into streets, blocks, and lots, and indicating the measurements of the individual parcels

plottage Increment in unity value of a plot of land created by assembling smaller ownerships into one ownership

points Discount charges imposed by lenders to raise the yields on their loans

police power The right of any political body to enact laws and enforce them, for the order, safety, health, morals, and general welfare of the public

power of attorney A written instrument duly signed and executed by a person that authorizes an agent to act on his or her behalf to the extent indicated in the instrument

prepayment clause A clause in a mortgage that gives a mortgagor the privilege of paying the mortgage indebtedness before it becomes due

price fixing Conspiring to establish fixed fees or prices for services or products

principal The employer of an agent or broker; the broker's or agent's client

probate To establish the will of a deceased person

purchase money mortgage A mortgage given by a grantee in part payment of the purchase price of real estate

Q

Glossary

quiet enjoyment The right of an owner or a person legally in possession to the use of property without interference of possession

quiet title suit A suit in court to remove a defect, cloud, or suspicion regarding legal rights of an owner to a certain parcel of real property

quit claim deed A deed that conveys simply the grantor's rights or interest in real estate, without any agreement or covenant as to the nature or extent of that interest, or any other covenants; usually used to remove a cloud from the title

R

racial steering The unlawful practice of influencing a person's housing choice based on his or her race

real estate board An organization whose members consist primarily of real estate brokers and salespersons

real estate syndicate A partnership formed for participation in a real estate venture; partners may be limited or unlimited in their liability

Glossary

realization of gain The taking of the gain or profit from the sale of property

real property Land, and generally whatever is erected upon or affixed thereto

Realtor A coined word that may only be used by an active member of a local real estate board, affiliated with the National Association of Real Estate Boards

reconciliation The final stage in the appraisal process when the appraiser reviews the data and estimates the subject property's value

recording The act of writing or entering in a book of public record affecting the title to real property

recourse The right to a claim against a prior owner of a property or note

redemption The right of a mortgagor to redeem the property by paying a debt after the expiration date and before sale at foreclosure; the right of an owner to reclaim the owner's property after the sale for taxes

redlining The refusal to lend money within a specific area for various reasons. This practice is illegal.

Glossary

referee's deed Used to convey real property sold pursuant to a judicial order, in an action for the foreclosure of a mortgage or for partition

release The act or writing by which some claim or interest is surrendered to another

release clause A clause found in a blanket mortgage that gives the owner of the property the privilege of paying off a portion of the mortgage indebtedness, and thus freeing a portion of the property from the mortgage

rem (See *in rem.)*

remainder An estate that takes effect after the termination of a prior estate, such as a life estate

remainderman The person who is to receive the property after the termination of the prior estate

rent The compensation paid for the use of real estate

reproduction cost Normal cost of exact duplication of a property as of a certain date

restraint of trade Business practices designed to restrict competition, create a monopoly, control prices, and otherwise obstruct the free operation of business

Glossary

restriction A limitation placed upon the use of property contained in the deed or other written instrument in the chain of title

reversionary interest The interest that a grantor has in lands or other property upon the termination of the preceding estate

revocation An act of recalling a power of authority conferred, as the revocation of a power of attorney; a license, an agency, etc.

right of survivorship Right of the surviving joint owner to succeed to the interests of the deceased joint owner; distinguishing feature of a joint tenancy or tenancy by the entirety

right-of-way The right to pass over another's land pursuant to an easement or license

riparian owner One who owns land bounding upon a river or water-course

riparian rights The right of a property owner whose land borders a natural watercourse, such as a river, to reasonable use and enjoyment of the water that flows past the property. Riparian literally means "riverbank."

Glossary

S

sales contract A contract by which the buyer and seller agree to terms of sale

satisfaction piece An instrument for recording and acknowledging payment of an indebtedness secured by a mortgage

second mortgage A mortgage made by a homebuyer in addition to an existing first mortgage

seizin The possession of land by one who claims to own at least an estate for life therein

setback The distance from the curb or other established line, within which no buildings may be erected

situs The location of a property

special assessment An assessment made against a property to pay for a public improvement by which the assessed property is supposed to be especially benefited

specific performance A remedy in a court of equity compelling a defendant to carry out the terms of an agreement or contract

Glossary

statute A law established by an act of the legislature

statute of frauds State law that provides that certain contracts must be in writing to be enforceable at law

statute of limitations A statute barring all right of action after a certain period from the time when a cause of action first arises

subagent An agent of a person already acting as an agent of a principal

subdivision A tract of land divided into lots or plots

subletting A leasing by a tenant to another, who holds under the tenant

subordination clause A clause that permits the placing of a mortgage at a later date that takes priority over an existing mortgage

subscribing witness One who writes his or her name as witness to the execution of an instrument

surety One who guarantees the performance of another; guarantor

surrender The cancellation of a lease by mutual consent of the lessor and the lessee

surrogate's court (probate court) A court having jurisdiction over the proof of wills, the settling of estates, and of citations

survey The process by which a parcel of land is measured and its area ascertained; also the blueprint showing the measurements, boundaries, and area

T

tax sale Sale of property after a period of nonpayment of taxes tenancy at will a license to use or occupy lands and tenements at the will of the owner

tenancy by the entirety An estate that exists only between husband and wife with equal right of possession and enjoyment during their joint lives and with the "right of survivorship"

tenancy in common An ownership of realty by two or more persons, each of whom has an undivided interest, without the "right of survivorship"

tenant One who is given possession of real estate for a fixed period or at will

Glossary

tenant at sufferance One who comes into possession of land by lawful title and keeps it afterwards without any title at all

testate Where a person dies leaving a valid will

tie-in arrangement A contract where one transaction depends upon another

title Evidence that owner of land is in lawful possession thereof; evidence of ownership

title insurance A policy of insurance that indemnifies the holder for any loss sustained by reason of defects in the title

title search An examination of the public records to determine the ownership and encumbrances affecting real property

Torrens title System of title records provided by state law; it is a system for the registration of land titles whereby the state of the title, showing ownership and encumbrances, can be readily ascertained from an inspection of the "register of titles" without the necessity of a search of the public records

Tort A wrongful act, wrong, injury; violation of a legal right

transfer tax A tax charged under certain conditions on the property belonging to an estate

Glossary

U

urban property City property; closely settled property

usury On a loan, claiming a rate of interest greater than that permitted by law

V

Valid Having force, or binding force; legally sufficient and authorized by law

valuation Estimated worth or price; the act of valuing by appraisal

variance The authorization to improve or develop a particular property in a manner not authorized by zoning

vendee's lien A lien against property under contract of sale to secure deposit paid by a purchaser

violations Act, deed, or conditions contrary to law or permissible use of real property void to have no force or effect; that which is unenforceable

voidable That which is capable of being adjudged void, but is not void unless action is taken to make it so

W

Waiver The renunciation, abandonment, or surrender of some claim, right, or privilege

warranty deed A conveyance of land in which the grantor warrants the title to the grantee

water rights The right of a property owner to use water on, under, or adjacent to the land for such purposes as irrigation, power, or private consumption

will The disposition of one's property to take effect after death

wraparound loan A new loan encompassing any existing loans

Glossary

Z

zone An area set off by the proper authorities for specific use; subject to certain restrictions or restraints

zoning ordinance Act of city or county or other authorities specifying type and use to which property may be put in specific areas

Index

Bibliography

BLUEPRINTS AND CONSTRUCTION DRAWINGS: A UNIVERSAL LANGUAGE. (2011, August 21). Retrieved from Construction53: http://www.construction53.com/2011/08/blue prints-and-construction-drawings-a-universal-language/

Chen, J. (2019, 23 2). *Investopia.* Retrieved from Triple Net Lease: https://www.investopedia.com/terms/t/triple-net-lease-nnn.asp

Chen, J. (2019, April 1). *Real Estate Definition.* Retrieved from Investopedia: https://www.investopedia.com/terms/r/realest ateagent.asp

Floor Plan Symbols. (n.d.). Retrieved from ED EDraw: https://www.edrawsoft.com/floor-plan-symbols.php

Gallett, R. a. (n.d.). *19 Extremenely Successful People who changed careers after 30.* Retrieved from Inc.com: https://www.inc.com/business-insider/people-who-found-success-and-changed-careers-after-30-years-old.html

How long do people stay in their home? (n.d.). Retrieved from Keeping Current Matters: https://www.keepingcurrentmatters.com/2017/08/07/how-long-do-most-families-stay-in-their-home-2/

Kashyap, S. (2019, June 24). *ProofHub.* Retrieved from Importance of Time Management in the Workplace: https://www.proofhub.com/articles/importance-of-time-management-in-the-workplace

LA County. (n.d.). Retrieved from www.lacounty.gov: https://www.lacounty.gov/business/

Marble, D. (n.d.). *Jeff Bezos Quit His Job at 30 to Launch Amazon--Here Are the 3 Simple Strategies He Used to Do It.* Retrieved from Inc.com: https://www.inc.com/darren-marble/jeff-bezos-quit-his-job-at-30-to-launch-amazon-heres-how-to-know-if-its-right-time-for-your-big-move.html

National Association of Realtors. (2018, May 11). Retrieved from Quick Real Estate Statistics: https://www.nar.realtor/research-and-statistics/quick-real-estate-statistics

NYC.gov. (n.d.). *Better Government Stronger Businesses.* Retrieved from www1.nyc.gov: https://www1.nyc.gov/assets/smallbizfirst/downloads/pdf/small-business-first-report.pdf

Occupational Employment and Wages, May 2018.
(n.d.). Retrieved from Bureau of Labor
Statistics:
https://www.bls.gov/oes/current/oes419022.ht
m#st

PAPPADEMAS, A. (2013, April 12). *Career Arc:
Harrison Ford.* Retrieved from Grantland:
https://grantland.com/features/harrison-ford-
career-arc/

QuickFacts. (n.d.). Retrieved from US Census
Bureau:
https://www.census.gov/quickfacts/fact/table/d
allascountytexas/SBO001212#SBO001212

Real Estate Brokers and Sales Agents. (n.d.).
Retrieved from Bureau of Labor Statistics:
https://www.bls.gov/ooh/sales/real-estate-
brokers-and-sales-agents.htm

Smith, J. (2019, June 25). Retrieved from
Investopedia:
https://www.investopedia.com/terms/b/broke
r.asp

Soniak, M. (2012, 10 17). *MentalFloss.* Retrieved
from Why are blueprints blue?:
http://mentalfloss.com/article/12797/why-are-
blueprints-blue

Chen, J. (2019, April 1). *Real Estate Definition.*
Retrieved from Investopedia:

https://www.investopedia.com/terms/r/realestateagent.asp

Smith, J. (2019, June 25). Retrieved from Investopedia: https://www.investopedia.com/terms/b/broker.asp

About the Author

Renowned as a foremost negotiations expert, George F. Donohue has been involved with more real estate negotiations than most real estate professionals in the world today.
He has managed one of the largest real estate portfolios in the world, which included being head of real estate for the World Trade Center in New York City.

Today, he is a corporate executive, author, professional speaker, consultant, professor, and television and radio spokesperson. Donohue has earned an associate's degree in construction management, a bachelor's degree in architecture, and a master's of science degree in real estate development at New York University.

Over his lifetime, Donohue has taught the business of real estate and the art of negotiation to thousands of people. He consults with corporations, governments, and individuals worldwide, and is sought out by the media for his knowledge of real estate, architecture, and business.

A well-known speaker-particularly in China, Japan, and Europe. His assignments have taken him to more than 40 countries around the globe. During his career, Donohue has negotiated against numerous top executives and individuals from entities such as the Japanese, Russian, and French governments, Merrill Lynch, Bank of America, Dean Witter, The Commodities Exchange, the Society of Security Analysts, The Gap, JPMorgan Chase, Citibank, HSBC, Marsh and McLennan, Daiichi Kangyo Bank, Allstate Insurance, Bank of Tokyo, Bank of Taiwan, Duane Reade, McDonald's, Charles Schwab, and hundreds of others.